WEAPON

M000290561

SNIPING RIFLES IN WORLD WAR I

MARTIN PEGLER

Illustrated by Adam Hook & Alan Gilliland

OSPREY PUBLISHING
Bloomsbury Publishing Plc
Kemp House, Chawley Park, Cumnor Hill, Oxford OX2 9PH, UK
29 Earlsfort Terrace, Dublin 2, Ireland
1385 Broadway, 5th Floor, New York, NY 10018, USA
E-mail: info@ospreypublishing.com
www.ospreypublishing.com

OSPREY is a trademark of Osprey Publishing Ltd

First published in Great Britain in 2022

A catalogue record for this book is available from the British
Library.

ISBN: PB 9781472850768; eBook 9781472850782;
ePDF 9781472850799; XML 9781472850751

22 23 24 25 26   10 9 8 7 6 5 4 3 2 1

Index by Rob Munro
Typeset by PDQ Digital Media Solutions, Bungay, UK
Printed and bound in India by Replika Press Private Ltd.

Osprey Publishing supports the Woodland Trust, the UK's
leading woodland conservation charity.

To find out more about our authors and books visit
www.ospreypublishing.com. Here you will find extracts, author
interviews, details of forthcoming events and the option to sign
up for our newsletter.

Dedication

To Major Tom, who did not live to see the publication of this
book, but for whose help I am truly grateful.

Author's acknowledgements

My grateful thanks to the many people who helped me with
information and images, in particular: Dr Bob Maze for
permission to use images; Dr Roger Payne for images from his
extensive collection; Steve Houghton for images from his seminal
work on British sniping; Morphy Auctions (www.morphy.
auctions.com) and Rock Island Auctions (www.rock.
islandauctions.com) for permission to use photographs from their
back catalogues; Lawrence Brown for much French material;
Barry Lees for the ammunition photographs; the World War I
snipers with whom I interviewed and corresponded, who
willingly shared their time and experiences; and to Katie, my
wife, for her forbearance while I wrote yet another book.

Editor's note

Unless otherwise noted, all illustrations are from the author's
collection.

Artist's note

Readers may care to note that the original paintings from which
the battlescenes in this book were prepared are available for
private sale. All reproduction copyright whatsoever is retained by
the publishers. All enquiries should be addressed to:

scorpiopaintings@btinternet.com

The publishers regret that they can enter into no correspondence
upon this matter.

Front cover, above: The Gew 98 bolt-action rifle – shown here
with 3× Emil Busch scope – had a five-round internal box
magazine and was clip-loaded using guide slots above the
receiver. The Gew 98 was superior in almost every respect to the
sniping rifles that British and Dominion forces were able to field
during World War I, which also meant that by the end of 1914
the German sniper was the most effective on the battlefield.
(Morphy Auctions)
Front cover, below: US Army snipers examine a Model 1903
Springfield with Warner & Swasey scope. (US Army)
Title-page photo: A very fine image of a pair of Austrian soldiers
sniping with a Mannlicher sporting carbine. Close examination
shows double-set triggers and the barrel is approximately 18in
long. Such carbines were normally chambered for the 6.5×54mm
Mannlicher round so it would be a competent weapon for short-
range shooting only.

CONTENTS

INTRODUCTION

World War I introduced numerous words into the English language. One such word is 'sniper'. Prior to 1914, however, this term was barely used, and anyone who was regarded as an above-average shot was referred to as either a marksman or sharpshooter (from the German term *Scharfschütze*, 'sharp-eyed shot'). It is not clear how the word sniper became a part of the English language, but the most likely explanation was its use by British officers in India in the 18th century, to describe the sport of game-shooting snipe, a fast and well-camouflaged bird that took considerable skill to shoot. The word may well have vanished without trace had it not been for the Anglo-Boer wars of the late 19th century, in which the frightening efficiency of Boer marksmen began to be reported by war correspondents as 'sniping'. When World War I broke out in July 1914, it rekindled memories of the southern African veldt in the minds of many British Army officers who had served there and reporters who had witnessed the conflict.

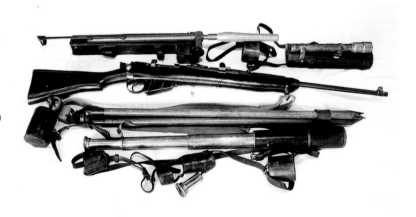

A unique survivor of the SMLE rifles used by Bailey's South African Sharpshooters, a unit expressly raised for sniping. The rifle has an Aldis scope in Purdey mounts and the front woodwork has been cut down to relieve pressure on the barrel, which affected accuracy. (James Winch)

In the first months of fighting on the Western Front a terrible toll was exacted by German riflemen on British and French troops holding the front lines. It was quickly realized that the accuracy of these shots striking men in the head was more than just sheer chance, as were the disproportionate numbers of officers killed. Suspicions were soon confirmed when killed or captured German riflemen were found to be equipped with telescopically sighted rifles – an innovation entirely unprecedented in European warfare. It soon became clear to the Allies that there were specialist units of German sharpshooters whose job was to target any unwary Allied soldier who momentarily exposed his head above the parapets of the newly dug trenches that had begun to snake across the countryside. This was not lost on the popular press in Britain, which once again began using officers' slang to describe the death of these men as being due to 'sniper fire'.

Since the American Civil War (1861–65), there had been no use of optically sighted rifles in warfare, and so none of the Allied armies of World War I had any concept of exactly what they were facing. Warning soldiers of the danger and ensuring that trenches were deeper and better protected with sandbags all helped the situation, but exactly what to do to combat this sniping menace was quite another matter. Britain had no rifles in military service with optical sights, but the Germans, due to their historical hunting traditions, had thousands of scoped commercial rifles that were pressed into use, as well as a manufacturing industry that was geared to producing military rifles with optical sights on a large scale.

While the British Army had a fine service rifle in the shape of the .303in Short, Magazine, Lee-Enfield Mk I, hereafter referred to as the SMLE, no provision was made for telescopic sights or specialized sniper training with it. The sole exception were the Canadians, who arrived in Britain in 1915 with some .303in Ross Mk III rifles equipped with Warner & Swasey M1913 scopes. Many other countries, such as France, Italy and the United States, initially paid scant attention to the increasing need for snipers and had to extemporize; others, such as Russia and the Ottoman Empire, never issued any telescopic-sighted rifles, relying on the shooting ability of competent soldiers.

So, at the start of the greatest conflict in human history, the combatants – with the exception of Germany and Austria–Hungary – entered into the war largely armed with very similar longarms, capable of reasonable accuracy and potential ranges in excess of 1,000yd, but with nothing in the way of optical systems or special training for sniping.

From being trench-based in the first three years of fighting, snipers would go on to become an integral part of the Allied offensives launched from 1917 onwards and for the Germans, a vital element in the defence of the battlefields as Allied pressure gradually forced them from the offensive onto the defensive. Sniper training courses on both sides began to include open warfare, street fighting and an increasing requirement for observation and intelligence-gathering. By November 1918, the sniper had taken his place among the most highly trained specialists on the battlefield and was the only infantryman equipped with a rifle specifically designed for his needs.

This German sniper carries minimal equipment, indicating that he is working from a front-line hide. The German Army sensibly decided to base its own sniping weapon on the issue rifle, the 7.92×57mm Mauser Gewehr 98 (Gew 98), and permitted any make of scope that met the requirements to be mated to a rifle using one of several mounting systems; this kept the supply and manufacture of such specialist rifles both cost-effective and controllable. Austria–Hungary followed suit, mating the 8×50mmR Repetier-Gewehr Modell 1895, otherwise known as the Mannlicher M95, with a variety of scope patterns, but using only two basic mounting systems.

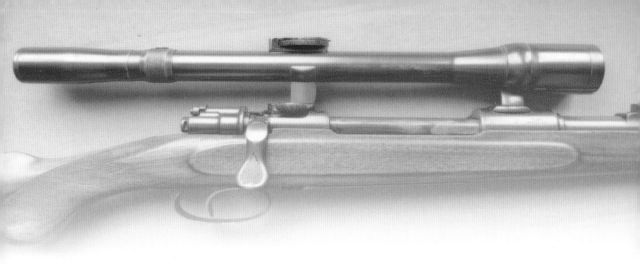

DEVELOPMENT
Rifles, scopes and mounts

A pre-war Mauser commercial rifle with a Zeiss scope. This is typical of the hunting rifles used by German snipers in the early months of World War I. Products of Germany's large commercial arms industry, these rifles were beautifully constructed, usually with fine walnut stocks, chequered to aid grip; the triggers were often of the double-set type, adjustable for pull. They were, however, sporting arms and not made with the durability required for front-line service. Barrels were comparatively short (22–26in) and light, being of relatively thin-walled construction to reduce the weight as most such rifles were lighter than the Gew 98, weighing less than 8lb. (Dr R. Maze)

GERMAN SNIPING RIFLES

While the infantry rifles issued by all combatants in World War I were broadly similar in type and performance, the technological leaders were undoubtedly the Germans, for the introduction in April 1898 of the Gew 98 provided the German Army with unarguably the world's strongest mechanical design of rifle.

Commercial hunting rifles

For the first months of the war, however, it was not military rifles that were to assist the German snipers in dominating no man's land, but large quantities of sporting rifles fitted with telescopic sights. Long range was not a prerequisite for these types of rifle as game shooting was normally conducted at 200–300yd. Official acknowledgement of this range limitation was underlined in a German Army pamphlet issued to snipers in 1915, which stated plainly that the weapons with telescopic sights were very accurate up to 300m (328yd).

Of course, Germany could not expect to wage a long war with snipers equipped solely with borrowed commercial rifles, which were available in a wide range of calibres, but the majority were chambered for the 7.92×57mm round, known as 'S-Munition' (*Spitzer*; pointed). While the old 8mm ammunition used before the advent of the current service round was still in plentiful commercial supply, it now posed a logistical problem for an army that was equipped solely with rifles that were designed to chamber the more powerful 7.92×57mm round. It was made clear that any sporting rifles issued to snipers at the start of the war were only safe to fire the old 8mm ammunition and in theory, each sporting rifle was fitted with a small engraved plate stating *Nur fur Patrone-88, Keine S-Munition Verwenden* ('only to be used with 8mm rounds, not suitable for S-Ammunition').

The Gew 98

The Gew 98 was an improved version of Germany's old Gewehr 88 rifle, with a rotating bolt using a unique triple-locking lug system, with two large main lugs at the bolt head and a third safety lug at the rear of the bolt, which served as a back-up in the unlikely case that either of the former two failed. The 29.1in-long barrel provided extremely good accuracy, although its length later proved a handicap in the close confines of trench warfare.

Within ten years of the introduction of the Gew 98, work had begun on designing a sniping variant. Adapting and fitting commercial patterns of mounts and scopes to create a military-issue sniping weapon was not difficult for the German Military Procurement Department; after all, Mauser sporting rifles had been fitted with scopes for decades. The system of selection for conversion was on the basis of test-firing all Gew 98 service rifles, which were expected to have an accuracy of one minute of angle (1 MoA) – equivalent to a 25mm or 1in group at 100m (109yd) – so any rifles that achieved a tighter grouping than this were deemed acceptable for sniping conversion. Perhaps one rifle in 100 might be deemed suitable and for this reason, sniping-variant Gew 98s will not be found within consecutive blocks of serial numbers. Nor is there any evidence that this practice changed throughout World War I, despite subsequent labour and component shortages within Germany's firearms factories.

The method of Gew 98 conversion was straightforward: a scope, rings and mounts would be sorted and loosely matched, as scope-body diameters often differed, each component then being stamped with an identical number (usually, but not exclusively with the last digit or two of the rifle's serial number) to ensure that they would remain together. These components were then passed to skilled military armourers, many of whom had been peacetime gunsmiths.

There were three primary forms of mount: a claw mount with a curved rear mount partially offset to the left to place the scope body overbore; an overbore claw mount with a bridge or aperture through the centre that provided a view of the iron sights; and a front claw with a post and locking catch at the rear, a mount pattern shared with many Austrian rifles. The Germans never employed the heavily offset scopes that the British did and their practice of always having the scope over the line of sight of the barrel was to prove a very important advantage in trench sniping.

Fitting the scope to the Gew 98 involved mounting a block at the front, normally with a dovetail for the scope base. The front block sat on the barrel Knox-form and a plain slotted block was attached to the rear of the receiver above the bolt. The rear mount could incorporate

A typical Gew 98 sniping rifle, with overbore claw mounts and an Austrian Kahles scope. (Rock Island Auctions)

THE GEW 98 EXPOSED

7.92×57mm Mauser Gewehr 98 with Oigee scope

1. Front sight
2. Front barrel band
3. Rear barrel band and sling swivel
4. Top handguard
5. Rear sight
6. Barrel
7. Chamber
8. Bolt handle
9. Safety catch
10. Cocking piece
11. Buttplate
12. Buttstock with rear sling attachment
13. Trigger
14. Trigger-guard
15. Rear sling swivel
16. Cartridges
17. Stock
18. Bayonet mount
19. Cleaning rod
20. Objective lens
21. Graticule
22. Elevation drum
23. Erector cells
24. Ocular lenses
25. Oigee telescopic sight body
26. Scope front mount
27. Scope body locking catch
28. Scope rear mount
29. Firing pin
30. Bolt body
31. Firing-pin mainspring
32. Rear trigger-guard screw
33. Sear
34. Front trigger-guard screw
35. Magazine follower
36. Magazine spring
37. Magazine floorplate
38. Magazine body

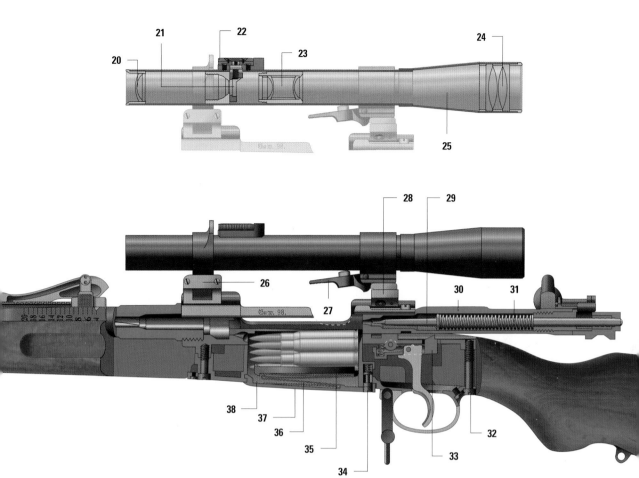

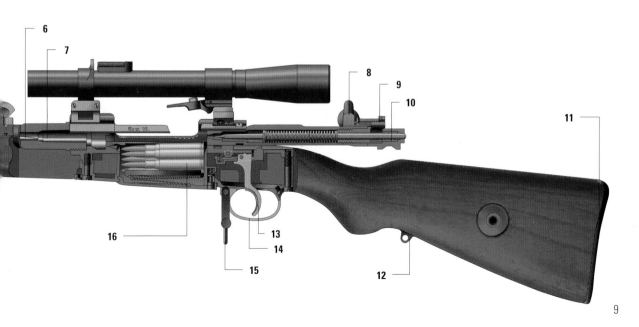

Adjustment on a Gew 98 sniping rifle. Adjusting the rear mount for windage involved using the small key supplied in the carry-case. The front dovetail could usually be moved laterally to duplicate this, but zeroing the rifle was very time-consuming.

either a spring-catch or lever that unlocked the rear claw and enabled the entire scope quickly to be lifted free of the rifle. Variations on this theme also existed, but all types of mounting system used were tried-and-tested patterns that had worked well on thousands of sporting rifles.

There was one problem inherent in using these mounting systems, however, and that was the difficulty in providing lateral adjustment, which at this time was not possible via the scope itself, as a turret design to allow windage adjustment was still a couple of decades away.

The only method available was by means of a winding screw on the rear base, which involved using a key to move the rear of the scope laterally, so the front base with its tight-fitting dovetail could be carefully tapped left or right to match any adjustment on the rear mount. Some front bases did not have this dovetail, so excessive rear adjustment could result in putting pressure on the scope tube, potentially twisting it out of line. As can be imagined, lateral adjustment of the scope was not an easy or desirable task to undertake once deployed in the front line and was the reason that each Gew 98 was factory set-up as accurately as possible in the first instance and why snipers were warned that all but the most basic adjustments required the Gew 98 to be returned to the armourer.

Each scope would be fitted into its rings, which were normally of a split-ring pattern with a screw to clamp them together, although there were some variants with one-piece or half-rings that required the scope to be secured with solder. The bases would be fitted to the Gew 98 using a jig and very carefully lined up to ensure they were perfectly parallel to the axis of the bore. Once satisfied, the armourer would drill and tap the holes in the Knox-form and rear receiver and fit the bases, which would be screwed and soldered into place and the scope attached.

Because the telescope had to be stripped of its internal components prior to soldering, it then had to be re-assembled. Often this setting-up also required the feet of the claw mounts to be carefully filed to ensure a perfect fit. The mounting system was extremely strong and did not require the Gew 98 to be zeroed every time the scope was dismounted – always the Achilles heel of any telescopic sight.

If at the final stage of the setting-up process a mistake was made and went unnoticed, it would result in an irreparably poor shooting rifle. In fact, because of slight manufacturing variations between the scopes, bases and rifles the Gew 98 suffered from a lack of interchangeability as one apparently identical scope and mount system would not necessarily fit onto the same bases of a different Gew 98, as the author can attest. Once the scope was mounted, the rifle was carefully re-assembled with the receiver carefully bedded into the stock, to ensure that it was as solid as possible and the bore and scope collimated. Some idea of the care taken can be gleaned from the fact that all visible screw heads on genuine German sniping rifles are either in line with, or at perfect right angles to the line of the bore. There was absolutely no practical point to this, but it was indicative of an age when craftsmanship was considered as important as the end result. Indeed, these screw heads were often covered over with a layer of solder to 'soldier-proof' them and were thus invisible.

The straight bolt arm also had to be modified by heating, bending it downwards in a jig to prevent it fouling the scope bell-housing when cocking the Gew 98, a modification eventually adopted on all later-model Gew 98a and Kar 98k rifles. Every rifle was then test-fired at ranges of 100m (109yd) increment, up to its maximum optical distance. Zeroing was usually undertaken at 300m (328yd) in 100m increments and the elevation dial marked accordingly.

A view of a partially offset Mauser claw mount, showing the steeply angled bolt handle and the carefully infilled screw holes. To provide a firm hold for the shooter, the inner face of the ball was ground flat and almost all Gew 98 sniping rifles will be found with a machined hollow on the stock next to the bolt handle to provide additional clearance for the fingers.

OPPOSITE
Some Mauser mounts had no method of adjusting the front scope base and the Gew 98 rifle had to be very precisely set up at the factory before being issued, as any subsequent movement of the rear mount could deform the scope body

11

GERMAN AND AUSTRIAN OPTICS

In 1846 Carl Zeiss opened a small workshop in the city of Jena in Thuringia, central Germany, for the manufacture of optical systems, and it was a natural collaboration when in 1884 he joined forces with Ernst Abbe and Otto Schott to form Glastechnische Laboratorium Schott & Genossen (Glass Technical Laboratory Schott & Associates), also based in Jena. There was a sound geographic reason for this location, for some of the best silicon dioxide (quartz) was available close-by in Austria. Zeiss had discovered that by means of a careful heating process, quartz mixed with calcium and an alkali would liquefy and if allowed to cool under very strictly controlled conditions produced glass with no bubbles, curvature or imperfections. The glass then had to be ground and polished, an exacting and very slow process entrusted only to skilled lens workers, but Germany and Austria had probably the largest such workforce in the world. The Germans and Austrians also pioneered the use of multiple lenses, for telescopes had until then had simple optical and objective lenses. They began to use multiple lenses known as an 'erecting cell' system, which improved magnification and lens sizes, resulting in far more efficient light transmission and a wider field of view.

In 1886 Ernst Abbe, a German optical scientist, began to collaborate with a chemist, Otto Schott, to try to perfect the complex science of manufacturing achromatic glass. Hitherto most glass suffered to some extent from coloured fringing around the image and a deterioration in image quality from the centre of the lens; this was termed chromatic aberration. By experimenting with different chemical compounds such as boron, barium and silicon, Schott managed to create several new forms of glass that were each suited to very specific purposes, such as microscopes, stellar telescopes and binoculars.

Sporting rifles prior to the 20th century had fixed brass-bodied scopes, zeroed to perhaps 150m or 200m (164–219yd) with elevation but no lateral adjustment, and a very narrow field of vision of about 2° or 3°. This posed a fundamental problem when used on a moving target, for the limited field of view meant that a running deer was only fleetingly visible through the scope and it was well-nigh impossible to take a snapshot using a telescopic sight. Nor did the small diameter of the tubes provide good magnification or sufficient vision in poor light conditions. It was not long, however, before the German optical industry was forging ahead in both the design and development of telescopic sights that were far more advanced than those in use anywhere else.

The new telescopic sights abandoned brass in favour of a strong one-piece tubular steel body, 20mm (0.79in) or 25mm (0.98in) in diameter and with a bell-shaped ocular end to which a leather eyecup was normally fitted to prevent unwanted ingress of light. As larger lenses were developed and employed they provided increased magnification, commonly 3× or 4×; and being of greater diameter, these lenses provided the shooter with a clearer sight picture, better field of vision and enhanced low-light vision than was offered by earlier lenses. The fact that these scopes could be used at far greater ranges than were usually required on a hunting rifle proved somewhat providential in view of the war clouds amassing on the horizons of Europe. By August 1914 there were at least 11 companies in Germany and Austria–Hungary producing good-quality telescopic sights: Bock, Busch, Feuss, Gerard, Goerz, Hensoldt, Oigee, Voigtlander and Zeiss in Germany, and Kahles and Reichert in Austria–Hungary.

During World War I, German telescopic sights were normally 3× or 4× with a range drum on the top body marked to 600m (656yd), 800m (875yd) or occasionally 1,000m (1,094yd). Most had a sliding focal plate, held by a screw, that enabled the focus to be adjusted for an individual shooter's eye, although a few manufacturers such as Gerard and Hensoldt had an adjuster ring in front of the ocular lens.

In theory, each scope was engraved with the serial number of its rifle, so that it would remain with that weapon for its service life. In practice, however, many scopes can be found un-numbered. They were supplied in fitted leather cases, with an instruction leaflet, a lens brush, a set of leather lens covers and a soft leather eyepiece.

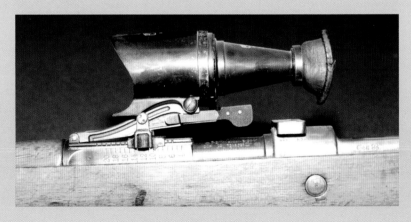

An early and rare example of a Zeiss auxiliary optical sight. Fitted to the standard rear sight of a service Gew 98, it was elevated by simply moving the sight-bed adjuster as normal, and was expressly developed to provide enhanced optics in poor light. The concept was years ahead of its time.

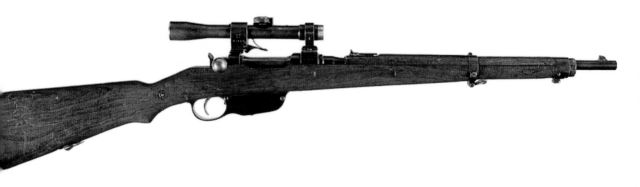

AUSTRIAN SNIPING RIFLES

Germany's staunch ally, Austria–Hungary, was also able to field good snipers, and the Habsburg Army had a tried-and-tested rifle in the form of the 8×50mmR Mannlicher M95. It shared with the Canadian Ross rifle (see pages 20–24) a complex straight-pull bolt design, using a rotating bolt-head in much the same manner as an artillery breechblock. The M95 itself was of typical late-19th-century pattern, long-barrelled at 30.1in with a five-round box magazine, but despite its somewhat old-fashioned appearance it proved to be a good, solid rifle for sniping conversion.

The selection of suitable M95s for conversion as sniping rifles was identical to that used by Germany for the Gew 98, but many converted M95s lack a bayonet bar. The method of scope mounting was slightly different, however. The bases were similar to those employed on German Gew 98 rifles, with a front pad on the Knox-form into which a single claw mount slotted. The rear base was a simple post-hole and both bases were curved, being slightly offset to the left. The scope had a sprung dismounting latch underneath its body, just forward of the rear base, which operated a spring-catch that released the rear of the scope, permitting it to be dismounted. As with the Mauser sniping models, some variations on a theme also exist, but this was the standard method employed by the Habsburg Army.

Both Austrian and German scopes can be found on M95 rifles, but unlike Germany, there were also carbine versions of the M95 converted for sniping. This may seem at odds with the requirements for a sniping weapon, but it must be borne in mind that much of the Habsburg Army was engaged in mountain warfare, where long, heavy rifles offering ranges of 800m (875yd) and beyond were unnecessary; shorter ranges of up to

An M95 sniping carbine fitted with a 3× Goerz scope. The release catch can be seen below the rear scope mount. (Rock Island Auctions)

An M95 sniping rifle fitted with a long Goerz telescopic sight and eyecup. The M95's very solid mounts made it a particularly robust sniping weapon. (Morphy Auctions)

A close-up of a 3× Goerz scope on an M95 sniping rifle. The range drum is graduated to 1,000m (1,094yd). All Goerz scopes had a distinctive protective bar across the front of the range drum. (Morphy Auctions)

400m (437yd) and portability were of greater consideration. Scope mounting followed the same type as on the long rifles, and a short pattern of scope manufactured by C.P. Goerz of Berlin is often found. Unlike the sniping conversions of the Gew 98, neither pattern of the M95 rifle had turned-down bolt handles as their design from the outset was shorter and consequently less likely to snag.

THE TURKISH MAUSER RIFLES

The Ottoman Army was supplied with several models of Mausers rifles: M1887, M1888, M1890, M1893 and M1903. All were variants on a theme and except for the M1887 (9.5×60mm black-powder loaded) and M1888 (7.92×57mm) were chambered for the 7.65×53mm round. They all employed the same basic Mauser locking system and the most commonplace patterns used in the fighting at Gallipoli in 1915–16 were the M1890 and M1893, the latter of which had a 29.1in barrel and which, because of Ottoman Army specifications, was manufactured of thicker steel than other export Mausers, providing superior accuracy. Unusually, the M1893 also had a magazine cut-off (as did the SMLE) and a slightly turned-down bolt handle. A standard-pattern metal ladder-type rear sight and blade front sight were fitted. It was inherently accurate and despite lacking a scope, it proved to be a remarkably good sniping rifle, much like the British Enfield P14.

An M1893 'Turkish Mauser' in 7.92mm calibre. This was one of several Mauser models used by the Ottoman Army, and despite its lack of optical sights, it proved a very competent sniping rifle. (Morphy Auctions)

SNIPING RIFLES OF THE BRITISH EMPIRE

It is fair to say that there were no telescopic sights available at the start of World War I that would enable British and Dominion riflemen to deal with the menace of German sniping. Nor were there any issue sniping rifles, capable of retaliating against the seemingly infinite numbers of German snipers and their loophole plates.

Commercial hunting rifles

In 1914, all that was available in limited quantities were commercially manufactured hunting rifles, produced by gunmakers such as Boss, Greener, Holland & Holland and Purdey & Sons. These were usually in large calibres – .450in, .500in or even .600in – that were able to smash through a loophole plate. Some were scoped but most were not, and they were expensive. In desperation the War Office sourced as many hunting rifles as they could – some 62 are on record as having been purchased – but many more were carried to the front by officers as personal rifles.

The SMLE

Introduced in 1904, the SMLE rifle was not radical in mechanical terms, for it used the same double-locking turning bolt-action common to practically all previous British military rifles of the period. What was different was that at 44.6in in length it was shorter than any other European service rifle. The British Army wanted a 'one-size-fits-all' long-arm rather than have to issue carbines, short and long rifles, as had been done in the past. The SMLE had a machined charger bridge to facilitate easy loading of two five-round stripper clips. It also acquired a very distinctive bayonet lug or stud that gave its muzzle a rather pugnacious appearance.

The new design not only succeeded in streamlining manufacture, thus reducing costs, but also proved itself to be an excellent combat rifle, suitable for all branches of the British Army. If the SMLE did suffer from any technical shortcomings, it was with the barrel, the wall of which was relatively thin, resulting in excessive harmonics (vibration) that adversely affected accuracy at long range. Nor was the composition of the steel used particularly hard, which limited barrel life; snipers were warned that shooting in excess of 500 rounds would cause wear that would noticeably affect accuracy. This is borne out by the fact that commercially manufactured Enfield target rifles had a heavyweight target barrel fitted. After some discreet testing by the Small Arms Committee at RSAF Enfield, in August 1904 it was found that altering the depth of the lead into the barrel provided some improvement in accuracy, but the SMLE Mk III was never to prove a favourite with long-range shooters. In practice for snipers, barrel wear or the fact that the SMLE could not match the longer-range accuracy of the Gew 98 was of little consequence, for even in the open warfare of the last year of World War I it was estimated in an official Canadian report that most sniping took place at distances between 150yd and 300yd.

The SMLE was issued to all British and Dominion forces, and it became the workhorse of the sniper companies, but how they were to meet the German snipers on their own terms was as yet an unsolved problem, for no telescopic-sighted rifles were available. The British Army's acquisition of a few big-game hunting rifles did nothing to stem the dominance of German snipers, but there did exist in large numbers and available to British and Dominion sharpshooters a small aiming device known as the Galilean sight. British and Dominion sharpshooters also used target-aperture sights, a particular favourite being the Parker-Hale No. 5 pattern, which had been specifically developed for competition use in conjunction with the Long Lee and SMLE rifles. These complex, fine-adjustable rear sights provided a sharp target image that an experienced rifleman could use effectively to 1,000yd. None of these devices really enabled Allied snipers to match the German snipers, however.

Clearly, some form of coherent response was required, and on 4 May 1915 the War Office issued Specification SA 390 for 'The fitting of telescopic sights to Rifle, Short, Magazine, Lee-Enfield Mk. III'. This was an open-to-all contract for any manufacturer or supplier able to produce or procure scopes and fit them to a service rifle; it was not intended to be a detailed specification for exactly what should be provided. The yawning gulf between what the British Army thought snipers needed and what they actually wanted is nowhere better illustrated than with Specification SA 390, for it made clear that all approved mounts and scopes had to be offset to the left, to enable charger-loading of the magazine. Thus, from day one, British snipers were handicapped by limited vision both literally and figuratively on the part of the War Office. One of the great champions of British sniping, big-game hunter and sniping devotee Major Hesketh V. Hesketh-Prichard, pointed out that it was impossible for a sniper so equipped to see through a loophole in a steel plate, given the narrowness of the aperture; all that could be seen was the inside of the steel plate (Hesketh-Prichard 1994: 87).

Nevertheless, the outcome was the tooling-up by three companies to equip the British Army with sniping rifles. These were the Periscopic Prism Company (PPCo) of London, Aldis Bros of Birmingham and Whitehead Bros, also of Birmingham. PPCo and Aldis Bros were already in the business of manufacturing optical sights, but Whitehead Bros provided mounts enabling the fitting of American Winchester scopes to the SMLE.

Of course, this was by no means the entire story, for very many other British gunmakers also provided scopes and mounts; these included J. Bartle & Co., W. Evans, D. Frazer & Co., Holland & Holland, W. Jeffrey & Co., Purdey & Sons, J. Rigby & Co. and E.R. Watts & Sons. Exactly how many of each type were manufactured is recorded in War Office contract documents, but the total for World War I appears to be 13,150 of all types, with PPCo providing the largest number – 4,072 – although several hundred PPCo telescopes were also fitted to rifles using alternative mounts supplied by many of the other companies such as Purdey & Sons, who produced some 1,400 conversions in 1915–16.

An early pairing of an SMLE Mk I rifle with an APX Mle 1916 scope. The weapon's origin is unknown, but early research indicates it may have belonged to Major Hesketh V. Hesketh Prichard. The rifle also has an aperture rear sight fitted. (Dr R. Maze)

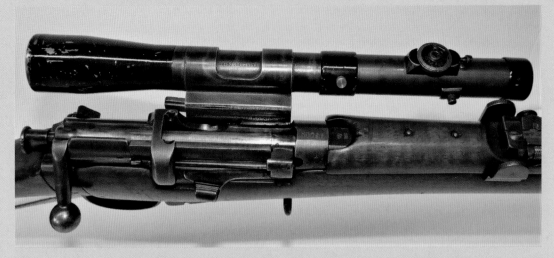

A PPCo scope on a 1918-dated SMLE. Despite some beliefs to the contrary, British sniping rifles were manufactured right up to the end of World War I. The left offset is very clearly shown, as is the size of the scope.

OPTICAL SIGHTS FOR THE LEE-ENFIELD

The **Galilean sight** utilized the simplest form of magnifying lenses, using no advanced technology and employing a large convex objective lens of about 1in diameter attached to the front sight of the rifle, with either a small concave ocular lens fitted on the rear sight or a fine-adjustable target aperture rear sight. There were five major manufacturers – Barnett, Gibbs, Lattey, Martin and Ulster/Neill – all of whom produced variations on a theme: the Martin and Ulster/Neill sights had an aiming dot on the objective lens; the Gibbs had a pointer and crosshair. In 1915 the War Office officially adopted the Ulster/Neill, Martin and Lattey types, the last of these

in the greatest number, some 9,000 being issued out of the 14,125 of all types purchased. In recent years, extensive testing undertaken by Dr Robert Maze, a lifelong collector of 19th- and 20th-century British weaponry, has revealed the likely performance of the Galilean sights in the hands of British and Dominion snipers (see pages 60–61).

The 2× **PPCo** scope was a large instrument, 12.25in in length and weighing a hefty 18oz, with a standard post and crosshair reticle. Two soldered rings around the scope body held a male block that slid onto a female dovetail that was screwed to the left of

The base mounting for a PPCo scope on an SMLE rifle. The front stop-plate was prone to shearing off and the somewhat weak locking spring could also cause accuracy problems.

A Winchester A5 scope on Whitehead mounts. The adjuster drums on the rear mount can be seen clearly. (Dr R. Payne)

the rifle's receiver. The scope could be dismounted using a rear-facing sprung thumb-latch. This design had its weaknesses in that recoil could cause the front face of the dovetail mount to shear its screws, as the weight of the scope slammed against it on firing, requiring an armourer to re-fit it, usually with solder and bigger re-threaded screws. The thumb-spring could also weaken, allowing the scope to move in its mount. The scope had the customary range drum on the top of the body, graduated from 100yd to 800yd, but suffered from an extremely fiddly method of deflection adjustment, requiring two metal posts to be unscrewed to move the post reticule to the left or right. There were no markings on the scope body to aid this process and it could only be done laboriously by trial and error.

The next largest producer of telescopic sights was Aldis Bros, a firm that manufactured 3,000 scopes, variously designated 1, 2, 3 and 4. Slightly more powerful than the PPCo scope at 3×, the **Aldis** scope was more compact at 10.8in in length, but was usually graduated to 600yd only. Most Aldis scopes were set-up in Purdey mounts, the rear mount having a lug that projected from the left of the receiver and located into a distinctive 'J'-shaped arm on the scope. Once in place, the front locking stud on the scope body was lowered into the mount, which had a post-hole with a locking latch. The Aldis scope was solid and unaffected by recoil, although typically offset to the left. One glaring anomaly was that the first three scope patterns actually had no deflection adjustment at all, so snipers using the Aldis became adept at judging sidewinds and deflection and aiming-off to compensate, which made shooting at longer-range targets quite challenging.

Winchester scopes were popular among pre-war civilian shooters and were widely available in the United States as the A3, A4 and A5 (the number denoting the magnification), the A5 having been introduced in 1910. They were distinctive in that they employed a pair of adjustable ring mounts which held the scope body rigidly by means of thumb-screws, which enabled the scope to be adjusted almost infinitely for range and deflection. Most examples found in British service were of the A5 type, but the slightly shorter 4× B4 model can also be found. The A-series scope body was some 16in in length and light at 6oz, but by military standards it was rather fragile, being made of thin steel tubing. This fragility was countered by the scope's additional magnification and ease of adjustment.

The scope mounts sat on dovetail bases that would under normal circumstances be mounted overbore on the rifle and work perfectly. The War Office did things its own way, however, so Whitehead Bros produced a simple offset mount that used a front 'L'-shaped angle bracket, with the male dovetail on it utilizing three screws to fix it to the left 'wing' protector of the rear sight. The rear base was also mounted with three screws, these being drilled and tapped into the front left wall of the receiver. The scope rings simply slid onto dovetails and were secured by thumb-screws. It was a relatively solid, simple system, although the front mount could be affected by the woodwork swelling in the wet and altering the zero; its ease of adjustment meant, however, that this could be compensated for when necessary.

An oddity of this pattern of mount was that after each shot, the scope moved forward under recoil and had to be manually pulled back, to use the artillery term, 'into battery'. This was not an insurmountable problem, but did make a rapid follow-up shot impossible. Had more A-series scopes been available, they may well have become the most formidable scopes of World War I, but Winchester was unable to meet the increasing wartime demand.

An Aldis 1 or 2 scope in Purdey mounts; a solid and well-designed set-up. The rifle is an early SMLE still fitted with its long-range volley sights. (S. Houghton)

An SMLE with an Aldis scope in Purdey mounts. The front block is soldered onto the barrel and the hooked scope mount locks onto an internal retaining bar, the scope then being held in place by a spring catch at the rear. This was a particularly solid pairing, the main drawback being the heavy offset to the left, as is clearly visible. The barrel and Knox-form would normally be covered by a modified wooden handguard. (Dr R. Payne)

The Ross rifle

In the case of Canadian soldiers who arrived on the Western Front in early 1915, their fighting was not conducted with the SMLE, but a Canadian-designed and -manufactured rifle that became notorious for the amount of criticism that was flung at it. The Ross rifle was a straight-pull design very similar to that of the Mannlicher M95, employing a rotating bolt housed in a sleeve within which were machined helical spirals, the bolt handle being integral with the sleeve. The bolt head had solid opposing locking lugs, rather like those on the breech of an artillery piece. This was expensive to machine and the cause of significant problems once the Ross was in front-line use. Canada's Minister of Militia and Defence, Sir Frederick W. Borden, was faced with a dilemma, however, as the Ross, although not yet accepted for military service, could be rapidly manufactured in large numbers whereas the SMLE was simply not available in quantity to Canadian soldiers. Understandably, Borden took the decision to adopt the Ross, so in 1903 it was issued as the Rifle, Ross Mk I. The rifle had a 28in barrel and very precisely manufactured iron sights calibrated to 2,200yd. The sights were adjustable for both elevation and windage.

A Ross M1910 rifle with a Warney & Swasey M1913 scope. The large eyecup is present, and the hole in it to prevent it sticking to the shooter can just be seen. (Rock Island Auctions)

OPTICAL SIGHTS FOR THE ROSS RIFLE

The Ross was the only rifle in Allied service to be equipped pre-war with a telescopic sight. Prior to 1914, the use of telescopes on sporting rifles in Canada was far more prevalent than in Britain, the opportunities for hunting being plentiful and both the types and quantities of game animals far greater than in Europe. The Canadian militia had examined a number of available sights, but settled on the American-made 6× Warner & Swasey M1908, designed by Ambrose Swasey and manufactured in Cleveland, Ohio. Modified 5.2× Warner & Swasey M1913 scopes were available in quantity, so 500 were ordered and 250 supplied between April and July 1915, the balance following in October 1916.

It should be noted that the M1913 was selected more as a matter of expediency than performance, for it had a number of inherent problems. It was a prismatic scope, which necessitated its rectangular body being both bulky and heavy, the scope and mount adding 2.5lb to the weight of the rifle. The scope body was very difficult to seal against moisture, which misted up the mirrors and lenses. The prism system was always problematical when used on a telescopic sight, for any tiny foreign body trapped inside is magnified. In addition, the M1913 was offset to the left, making it awkward to use; worse, from the point of view of the sniper, it suffered from an extremely short (1.5in) eye-relief, the ocular lens

having a heavy rubber eyecup fitted to protect the eye socket from potential damage caused by recoil. Tales of the eye-cup adhering to the sniper's eye socket due to suction, while doubtless exaggerated, have a ring of truth to them as there are holes in the rubber body to prevent this. In fact, the mounting system actually had two positions, to provide an optional eye-relief setting – which in view of the M1913's reputation was probably a sensible idea.

There were troubles too with the mounting plate on the left side of the receiver, which carried the fitting screws on firing, causing loosening and play to appear. The remedy, mentioned by Canadian sniper Herbert W. McBride of the 21st (Eastern Ontario) Battalion CEF, was to tap tiny pieces of razor blade into the gap, wedging it solid – much to the disgust of the armourers, who found them almost impossible to remove.

In its favour, the M1913 provided the greatest magnification power of any military scope of the day – although its magnification restricted its field of view to 4.5° – and adjustments were easily made using a large elevation dial, optimistically graduated to 3,000yd and a windage dial marked in ten-unit increments. It speaks volumes for the Ross/M1913 combination that Canadian snipers were to become the most aggressive and successful of the whole war, outperforming even the Germans.

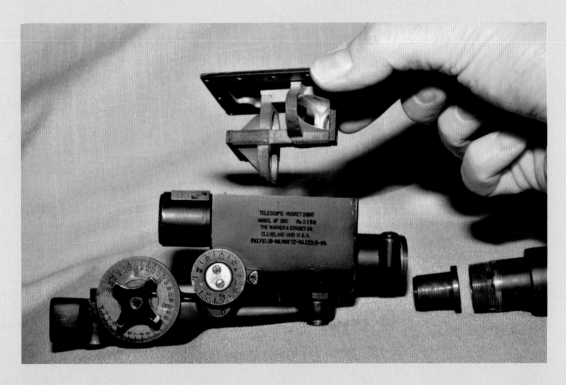

The prismatic lens assembly dismounted from a Warner & Swasey M1913 scope; its complexity is evident and the multiple lenses caused endless problems in combat.

THE ROSS RIFLE EXPOSED

.303in Ross M1910 Mk III rifle with Warner & Swasey M1913 scope

1. Buttstock
2. Cocking piece
3. Rear sight
4. Warner & Swasey M1913 scope
5. Receiver
6. Top handguard
7. Barrel
8. Front sight
9. Front barrel band, swivel and bayonet lug
10. Rear barrel band and swivel
11. Cartridge in chamber
12. Magazine
13. Trigger-guard
14. Trigger
15. Rear sling swivel
16. Receiver screw, rear
17. Yoke and yoke roller
18. Safety
19. Charger-guide base
20. Bolt
21. Firing-pin mainspring
22. Firing pin
23. Receiver screw, front
24. Link (right)
25. Magazine-spring plunger
26. Magazine spring
27. Magazine floorplate
28. Pawl
29. Pawl spring
30. Sear spring
31. Sear

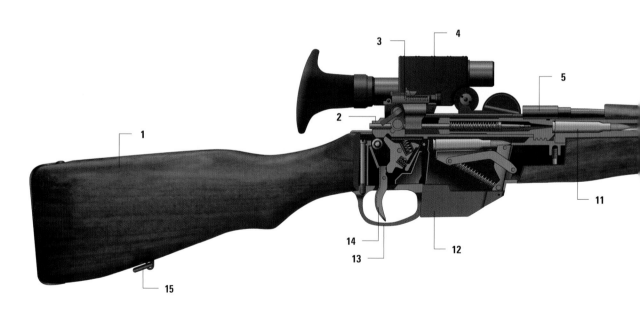

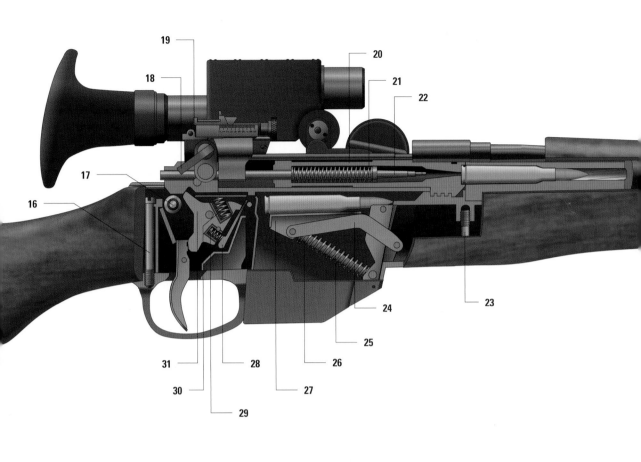

As far as calibre was concerned, most Ross rifles were initially chambered for the very potent .280in Ross round introduced in 1906; with a 140-grain bullet it was capable of an impressive muzzle velocity of 3,000ft/sec. It was no coincidence that the British had been experimenting with a near-identical .276in round; but in a wartime economy there was no way that Canada could countenance introducing a different calibre, so all Ross Mk I and Mk II rifles intended for military use were chambered for the .303in Enfield round.

The Ross was an exceptionally accurate rifle and gained a huge following among target shooters, and it soon began to dominate the long-range competitions; at the 1913 Camp Perry competitions the Ross virtually swept the board. Its subsequent failure as an infantry rifle is not within the scope of this book; suffice to say that in the prevailing trench conditions in World War I it performed badly. The problem lay partly with low-quality wartime ammunition, but also with the rifle's inherently weak extractor and the poor design of bolt stop. In addition, the inability of soldiers to keep the vulnerable locking lugs free of mud and dirt led to excessive force having to be used to open or close the bolt. The end result was the withdrawal of the Ross as an infantry rifle in September 1916, soldiers being supplied with the SMLE instead. Even so, Canadian Expeditionary Force (CEF) sniper units that wished to could and did retain many hundreds of Ross rifles, usually distinctively modified by the removal of the warp-prone forend, and they provided excellent service, many being re-issued in World War II.

The P14 rifle

Aside from the SMLE, one other British-manufactured rifle that saw service as a sniping rifle in World War I was the Enfield Pattern 1914 Mk I*F, a design based largely on the Mauser action. Although tested pre-war as the Pattern 1913 rifle, chambering the advanced .276in (7mm) round, the rifle proved impractical to put into production in any calibre other than .303in under wartime constraints. The P14 was quicker to manufacture than the SMLE and was rushed into production at the beginning of the conflict; a simplified model was introduced in June 1916.

The P14 was an exceptionally accurate rifle, partly because of the heavier five-groove barrel, but mainly due to the excellent iron sights fitted. The rifle had a fine-adjustable ladder-type rear sight and a barleycorn front sight as well as the long-range dial sight fitted to earlier Enfields, although the latter was later dispensed with.

Although the P14 was not generally liked by ordinary infantrymen as it was not as well balanced as the SMLE and held only five rounds in its internal magazine, it was adopted by most of the British sniper training schools as it was regarded as being just as accurate as a scope-equipped rifle, albeit without the advantages of magnification. Inevitably, a sniping variant was developed, the Mk I*W(T) with various patterns of scope, primarily Aldis or PPCo, and ostensibly accepted into service for sniping in April 1918. Production problems meant that supplies of the rifle were not available until just after the war had ended, however. Many thousands were placed into store, and hurriedly issued on the outbreak of World War II in 1939.

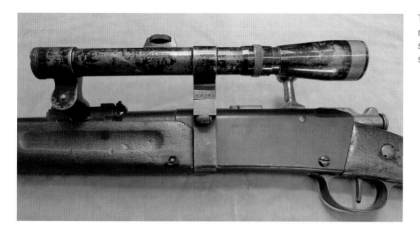

FRENCH SNIPING RIFLES

In 1914 France's armed forces were still using the venerable 8×50mmR Fusil d'infanterie Mle 1886 Lebel rifle, which was an outmoded design that employed an old-fashioned tubular magazine. Moreover, the bolt action of this rifle was long and the straight bolt handle awkwardly placed, making loading and cocking a cumbersome procedure. Allied to the tubular magazine, the heavy barrel, which at 31.5in was 7in longer than the SMLE's, made the Lebel both muzzle-heavy and clumsy. If that was not sufficiently problematic, the use of an acutely bottlenecked cartridge meant that any future weapon development would require a banana-shaped magazine to allow for the shape of the cartridge, or a completely new design of round.

The length of the Lebel, exacerbated by the fitting of its long, cruciform bayonet, made it very impractical for trench fighting, but so many had been manufactured that it remained the front-line infantry rifle for France's armed forces throughout World War I. It was not actually a bad weapon, being tough, simple and reasonably accurate – an ordinary production example was expected to achieve a group of 2 MoA at 100m (109yd) – but none of its deficiencies were lost on the Ordnance Department, which by 1914 realized that the Lebel had reached the end of its useful service life. From 1915 the French started to introduce the 8×50mmR Fusil d'infanterie Mle 1907/15 transformé, or Berthier. Unfortunately, this weapon had a mere three-round magazine capacity due to the design of its cartridge.

In the face of terrible casualties suffered at the hands of German snipers in 1914, the Ordnance Department was convinced by French Army field commanders that some method of retaliation was vital. That the Lebel rifle should be chosen was preordained, for what else was there available in sufficient quantity? Neither the Lebel nor the Berthier were to prove particularly effective sniping rifles, but the reality was that the numbers issued were relatively small, allocation apparently being six to eight sniping rifles per battalion. There is some evidence too that, as in Germany, sporting rifles were used as *pro tempore* sniping rifles, *la chasse* ('the hunt') being as fundamentally important to French rural life as it was to the Germans. Although very few of these rifles would have been optically equipped, there were certainly enough good-quality weapons in circulation to provide a better tool for sniping than the issue Lebel.

FRENCH OPTICAL SIGHTS

Once the Lebel rifle had been selected for sniper use a suitable optical sight was required. The sole candidate was the simple 2.5× telescopic sight fitted to the 37mm TRP (*tir rapide* ('rapid fire'), Puteaux) Mle 1916 infantry field gun: the LVM (*lunette viseur Mignon*; Mignon telescopic sight) manufactured by Manufacture d'armes et de cycles de Saint-Etienne (MAS). The LVM sight was viable for several reasons: the lenses were available in relatively large quantities; its optical properties were well understood; its power could be increased for sniping use; and production of the scope bodies could be modified fairly quickly to enable them to be fitted to the Lebel Mle 1886/93 and the Berthier Mle 1907/15 and

A Lebel M1886/93 sniping rifle fitted with an APX Mle 1917 scope, which was even more offset than the scopes on British rifles.

1916 rifles. So, in early 1916 the French ordnance workshops at Puteaux, near Paris were instructed to expand production of TR Ateliers de construction de Puteaux scopes (generally abbreviated to APX) and to modify them appropriately to turn them into workable sniping scopes. Unfortunately, there is no known documentation surviving that covers the manufacture or production of these sights, but the first pattern produced, the APX Mle 1916, appears to have been issued in mid-1916.

The 3× APX Mle 1916 was calibrated out to 800m (875yd), measured 9.5in in length and weighed 1.5lb. Elevation was controlled by means of a top-mounted rotating dial and windage was adjusted by means of a grub-screw on the front body of the scope, enabling the objective lens to be rotated in the manner of the British PPCo scopes; although this was fiddly, it was easier to adjust than its British counterpart. The reticule had a fine crosshair with a field of view of about 7° and a focusing ring just forward of the ocular lens. Although subject to parallax problems, they were well-constructed scopes with excellent optics. Unusually for this period, the entire scope body was made from heavy drawn-brass tube, the only steel fittings being the mounts. The mounts were strong and 'soldier-proof', the front mount having a side-mounted circular base soldered on the left side of the barrel near the rear sight, into which the circular stud of the front scope mount fitted. The rear mount had a simple slotted block at the rear next to the breech, with a thumb-latch release.

An improved version, the 3× APX Mle 1917, was slightly longer-bodied at 11in, but aside from providing a marginally better quality of image for the sniper it was otherwise identical to the APX Mle 1916, although some models appear to have an inverted-'V' reticule in place of the crosshair. The Mle 1917's mounting method was very different, however, utilizing a clamp on the breech of the rifle and a threaded thumb-screw to the rear, making it easier to dismount. Exactly why the Mle 1917 was produced is not clear, however, other than because its mounting system was easier to manufacture and fit than that of the Mle 1916, and it may simply have been a means of increasing production of telescopic sights at a time when French industry was under very great pressure.

As with all telescopic sights of this period, every rifle was hand-fitted with its scope by skilled gunsmiths or armourers in the slow assembly process of the period, and every scope was marked with the serial number of its rifle. Interestingly, unlike British optical sights, French scopes of the same pattern generally seem to have been interchangeable.

While this manufacturing process was under way the French Army acquired a few American Winchester A5 scopes, but whether this was by special arrangement or simply through commercial purchase is not known. From late 1914 some were fitted to Lebel rifles, examples today being exceedingly rare.

A Filotecnica scope for the Carcano rifle. The simple ring mounts and rear adjusting screws are similar to those of the Winchester A5, but the recoil spring to return the scope to its viewing position was an innovation. The Filotecnica scope employed two blocks screwed to the receiver of the Carcano rifle, but with two mounting rings as found on the Winchester A5 scope, within which the scope body sat, the rear mount having two screw adjusters to provide both elevation and lateral adjustment. As with the A5, the Filotecnica scope slid forwards under recoil, but was fitted with a spring to pull the scope back into battery after each shot.

ITALIAN SNIPING RIFLES

During World War I, Italy's dedicated sniping rifle was based upon the Fucile Modello 1891 rifle, more commonly known as the Carcano. The basic rifle design was like many others, sound but unexceptional, with an action based on the Mauser design and a six-round clip-loading system taken from the Mannlicher M95. The Carcano rifle had a barrel length of 30.7in and the Moschetto carbine, 18in. Like their Austro-Hungarian counterparts, the Alpini, the Italian Army's mountain troops, sometimes carried the carbine variant in preference to the long rifle and like the Mannlicher M95 it proved to be adequate for relatively short-range sniping.

Where the Carcano was unusual was in its use of gain-twist or progressive rifling, which has an increasing rifling twist as it progresses towards the muzzle. This theoretically imparts a smoother momentum to the bullet and reduces its tendency to drift in the direction of the twist. This type of rifling was rarely found in small arms because of the cost and complexity of manufacture, yet oddly the Carcano was chambered for the underwhelming 6.5×52mm round.

An Italian sniper with his observer, somewhere on the Isonzo Front. Surviving photographs show the Carcano rifle to have been equipped with a mix of sights: French-made APX scopes, some American-made Winchester patterns and German (or more probably Austrian) commercial scopes. For the long ranges that were possible in the mountains, the lower-power optics were inadequate, so from early 1916 a Milan-based optical company, La Filotecnica, produced a side-mounted 4× scope, shown here.

27

SNIPING AMMUNITION

In the late 19th century the military-rifle bullets in use in most countries were heavy solid-lead patterns, with long parallel bodies, flat bases and round noses, propelled by large charges of black powder. These, it was believed, provided the best combination of stability, accuracy and stopping power – but in 1884, everything changed.

In **France**, the invention in 1882–84 of smokeless powder led to the introduction of a new small-calibre, high-velocity 8×50mmR round into French military service in 1886. It was loaded with the new smokeless powder, 'Poudre B', but crucially it was soon also to be fitted with an entirely new type of pointed, tapered bullet designed by Capitaine Georges R. Désaleux in 1898. Tests showed that these pointed bullets created a much smoother airflow and the taper, or boat-tail, at the rear resulted in a swirl of air that reduced drag and improved long-range performance. Early concerns over the lack of lethality of these smaller-calibre bullets proved unfounded, for after extensive testing it was shown that far from being less efficient when striking a human body, use of the new bullets resulted in wounds of increased severity, as the higher energy and terminal velocity led to tumbling upon impact.

The military Lebel bullet adopted in 1899 weighed 198 grains and generated a muzzle velocity of 2,380ft/sec. Moreover, it was uniquely manufactured from lathe-turned 90/100 brass; but this advanced new ammunition was to create more problems than it solved when used in conjunction with the Lebel rifle. While round-nosed bullets were fine for tubular magazines, the new spitzer design caused incidents in which the bullet nose struck the primer of the round in front, detonating it. The heavily tapered and bottlenecked case design meant that the rounds lay nose-down in the magazine tube; an annular ring on the base of each cartridge was supposed to help protect the point of the bullet from accidentally striking the primer of the round in front. As became evident with the Berthier rifle, however, changing to a rifle with a box magazine meant that any more than a three-round capacity required an impractical magazine to allow for the ammunition curvature. The French Army had little option but to continue to use the Lebel ammunition; but there was no doubt that despite its exterior design limitations, the Lebel bullet's performance was certainly superior to all others – as evidenced by the interest German and British ammunition designers took in it.

This French development shook the armed forces of **Germany**, who hitherto had been happily using the old round-nosed Patrone 88. This round weighed 226 grains and produced a muzzle velocity of 2,854ft/sec. In 1905 the German Army adopted a new standard round loaded with smokeless powder, the 7.92×57mm *Spitzgeschoss Patrone* ('pointed bullet cartridge'); this bullet pattern was subsequently universally referred to as the 'spitzer'. At 154 grains the bullet was lighter by almost half compared to the old 8mm round, and it attained a velocity of 2,891ft/sec. The combination of weight and velocity resulted in a flatter trajectory and increased range – both very desirable elements to snipers.

This ammunition, it should be stressed, was for general issue and was not produced specifically with sniping in mind. Indeed, no special sniping ammunition was manufactured during 1914–18 by any country. There was, however, a special-purpose round produced that was to become of practical use to German snipers: the 178-grain tungsten steel-cored *Spitzgeschoss mit Stahlkern* (SmK; 'pointed bullet with steel core') armour-piercing round, which was able to penetrate almost any sheet steel of the period and was issued from mid-1915 in limited quantities to German snipers. There was another round developed, a heavy ball officially called the *schweres Spitzgeschoss* or *sS Patrone* ('heavy pointed bullet cartridge') that weighed 197 grains; although its velocity was slightly slower, at 2,575ft/sec, it had much-increased penetrative power due to its extra weight. Rather fortunately for the Allies, it was introduced only in the final months of World War I, with hardly any seeing sniper service. It was later to become the foremost German sniping round in World War II.

Realization had also dawned in **Austria–Hungary** that the Habsburg Army needed to update its old 8×52mmR black-powder-loaded ammunition. As an interim measure the Austro-Hungarians adopted an 8×50mmR smokeless round designated the M1888/90, and improved it to produce the M93 *Scharfe-Patrone*. Oddly, they opted to retain the round-nosed design of the old nickel-jacketed bullet, which meant that the 244-grain bullet was slower than most others, at 2,035ft/sec when fired from the M95 rifle; if used in conjunction with the M95 carbine, it was even slower still at 1,950ft/sec. Armour-piercing ammunition was developed in Austria–Hungary in 1908 and it utilized a spitzer design. Its penetrative power was slightly less than that of the German round, and it is not known whether it was issued in any quantity to snipers.

The armed forces of the **Ottoman Empire** actually had a better-performing round than Austria–Hungary, in the form of the 7.65×53mmR Mauser. The original 1889 military ball ammunition introduced for use in the Mauser M1893 rifle was loaded with a 210.7-grain round-nosed bullet that attained a muzzle velocity of 2,133ft/sec; but it was obvious through testing that this type of bullet was nowhere near as efficient as the new French 'Balle D' spitzer design, so Mauser followed the French lead in producing a 7.65mm pointed bullet that weighed 154.3 grains and had a muzzle velocity of 2,723ft/sec.

Shortly afterwards, a heavier 7.65mm bullet in the shape of the 173.6-grain spitzer was introduced; it had a muzzle velocity of 2,379ft/sec and belatedly copied the Lebel bullet in having a tapered rear (boat-tail) that provided even greater streamlining and range. To give some idea of how great the improvement was, the spitzer increased the maximum range from the older round's 3,700m (4,046yd) to 5,000m (5,468yd).

In **Britain**, the .303in Enfield Mk VI round, originally loaded with a 215-grain round-nosed bullet, had not proven reliable at extended range, so in October 1911 a new 174-grain spitzer bullet, the Mk VII, was approved for service. (Despite some assertions that at this point the British Army adopted a boat-tailed bullet similar to the Lebel bullet, this was never the case; it was not brought into service until adopted as the Mk VIII Z in July 1939.) The standard-issue Mk VII round was able to penetrate 9in of bricks, 14in of mortar or 18in of hard-packed sandbag at 100yd, almost identical performance to the Mauser bullet.

What Britain lacked was any special-purpose types of ammunition. Before 1914 the British Government had employed the giant Austrian ammunition-making company, Georg Roth, to develop an armour-piercing bullet. Roth duly produced a 174-grain bullet with a plain-steel core, but in tests it proved to be only a little more effective than an ordinary ball round and was not accurate at long range. In mid-1916 the ammunition maker G. Kynoch & Co. of Birmingham came up with an improved design, the 170-grain Mk VII P, but this too proved problematical, being difficult to manufacture as well as inaccurate, due to the hard core preventing the overly thin copper envelope of the bullet from gripping the rifling sufficiently. The answer lay in fractionally increasing the diameter of the bullet and this solved the problem so effectively that the newly designated Mk VII S round remained in service for almost 40 years. The Mk VII S was not issued in any quantity until mid-1916, however, and then mostly for aviation service, so most British snipers probably never even knew of its existence.

What was available to British snipers was the .303in Enfield Mk I L tracer round, known as 'Flame Tracer'. This early (pre-1914) pattern was identical in weight to the ball round, but suffered from numerous problems – including a failure to ignite – and by late 1916 a new tracer round, the Mk VIII GL, was introduced. Breaking with tradition, it had a lighter (158-grain) bullet that did not have any long-range capability, but this mattered little as the tracer compound burned out after a fairly short flight time. More troublesome was its lighter bullet, which meant that a scope zeroed for ball ammunition had to be re-zeroed. Mostly, the Mk VIII GL was relegated to target spotting, the user marking the position of a concealed enemy machine gun or sniper and thereby allowing British machine guns or field artillery to deal with the problem. Both incendiary and explosive ammunition were reserved for aviation use and such rounds were never issued to British infantry.

Despite producing a relatively high muzzle velocity of 2,296ft/sec, the 6.5×52mm Carcano rifle round used by **Italy** had a light (162-grain) bullet. This meant that the bullet lost velocity very quickly, falling to a subsonic 1,126ft/sec after a mere 300yd, rendering it ineffectual against steel plate, thick sandbags parapets and other obstacles.

Through hard combat during the Philippines War (1899–1902) the **United States** had realized that the original .30-40 Krag round lacked performance, so in 1906 a replacement was adopted in the form of the more powerful .30-06 Springfield round. It propelled a 150-grain flat-based spitzer bullet at a muzzle velocity of 2,700ft/sec and with minor modifications, remained the US military standard until the introduction of the 7.62×51mm NATO round in 1954. In World War I, the United States issued no special-purpose ammunition for sniping use, a situation that did not change until the Vietnam War (1955–75) when M118 Special Ball ammunition was introduced.

The most commonly used military ammunition of World War I. From left: the 6.5mm Carcano, 7.65mm Turkish Mauser, 7.92mm Mauser, 8mm M95 Mannlicher, 8mm Lebel, .303in Enfield Mk VII, .30-06 Springfield.

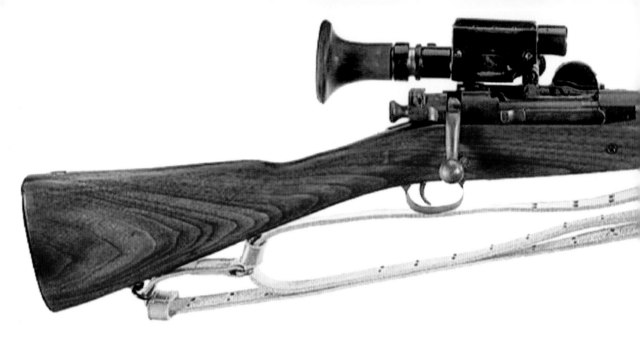

A Springfield Model 1903 rifle fitted with a Warner & Swasey M1913 scope. The short length of the Model 1903, similar to that of the British SMLE, is very clear. (Rock Island Auctions)

US SNIPING RIFLES

The Springfield Model 1903 rifle

When the American Expeditionary Forces began to arrive in France in the spring of 1917, they were armed with the 'US Magazine Rifle, Caliber .30, Model of 1903', known to the wider world as the Springfield Model 1903. Like the British SMLE, the design of which influenced it, the Model 1903 was a compromise in terms of length with its 24in barrel, but it had proven itself to be a reliable and accurate infantry rifle.

A pressing problem facing the American Expeditionary Forces' commanders was their inability to field any trained snipers, or many telescope-equipped rifles for that matter, despite the US Chief of Ordnance having published a report in 1903 on the .30-40 Krag-Jørgensen rifle, recommending that it be fitted with a telescopic sight. With the subsequent adoption of the new rifle, these recommendations were amended to include the Springfield Model 1903. This was all very well in theory, but the Ordnance Department did not regard this as a priority, nor did they actually have a suitable scope in mind to adopt.

The selection process for rifles to be converted for sniping use was identical to that adopted by other countries: production rifles were test-fired, accurate examples set aside and the muzzles stamped with a star mark to ensure easy future identification. Each individual scope was mated to each individual rifle and numbered to match. The scopes were issued with strict instructions that each was to remain only on that specific rifle, although in practice, unlike most other optical systems of the period, they were usually interchangeable.

OPTICAL SIGHTS FOR THE SPRINGFIELD MODEL 1903

All that was readily available to the US Army was the then-experimental Warner & Swasey M1908, which suffered from all of the shortcomings already mentioned, but inexplicably the US Army followed the British practice of using an offset mount, as it too believed charger-loading was a vital function for a sniping rifle. Several examples of the Model 1903 rifle were converted for testing at the Springfield Armory in Massachusetts, by means of manufacturing a male dovetail base that required the drilling and tapping of three screws into the left-hand side of the receiver and then screwing the dovetail base in place. The scope was then fixed in place by sliding the female mount onto it; locking was achieved by means of a spring-loaded plunger. It is worth noting that at around $80 each, these scopes were double the cost of a Springfield Model 1903 rifle. In spite of this, testing proved the scope to be acceptable, and by 1912 the US Ordnance Department had ordered some 2,075 of the newer 6× Warner & Swasey M1908 scopes; but the myriad problems besetting that model resulted in delays to production and the eventual introduction of yet another Warner & Swasey model, the 'Musket Sight, Model of 1913'.

The M1913's magnification was reduced to 5.2×, which increased the light-gathering properties of the scope and provided a brighter image; sealing against moisture was also improved, but otherwise it was remarkable for retaining all of the deficiencies of

the original M1908 scope. Despite some 5,730 of the M1913 having been produced by the end of World War I, it has been estimated from surviving serial numbers that probably no more than 1,530 were ever mounted to rifles for service use.

If the US Army was in dire straits, then so too was the US Marine Corps. The Marines also made use of the Model 1903 and because of the emphasis they placed on accurate shooting, had been looking pre-war for an effective telescopic sight that could be used for their competitive-match rifles. They were unimpressed by the Warner & Swasey scopes and turned their attention to the Winchester A5; by 1911 a few Model 1903s had been fitted with them. Sensibly, the Marines saw no good reason to fit the scopes anywhere but overbore, so they were mounted on a pair of standard commercial dovetail bases, one on the Knox-form and the other just forward of the rear-sight platform. In 1917, to prevent the scopes loosening on their blocks, tapered 'Mann' bases were procured by the US Marine Corps and fitted to selected rifles. When the Marines eventually arrived in France, however, only a very few scoped rifles came with them, possibly numbered in the dozens; a drop in the ocean compared to the numbers actually needed. US Army and US Marine Corps snipers used the iron sights of their issue rifles, and made the best they could of them, many achieving very creditable tallies as a result.

THE MODEL 1917 ENFIELD EXPOSED

.30-06 Model 1917 Enfield rifle

1. Butt plate
2. Buttstock
3. Cartridge in chamber
4. Top handguard
5. Lower barrel band with sling swivel
6. Upper barrel band with sling swivel
7. Barrel
8. Front sight
9. Bayonet lug
10. Stock
11. Cartridges
12. Trigger
13. Trigger-guard
14. Rear sling swivel
15. Rear-sight aperture
16. Rear-sight slide

17. Rear-sight slide catch
18. Rear-sight guard
19. Battle sight
20. Cocking piece
21. Sear notch
22. Firing-pin mainspring
23. Bolt
24. Striker
25. Extractor collar
26. Front guard screw
27. Feed ramp
28. Magazine follower
29. Magazine spring
30. Interlock slot
31. Sear spring
32. Floor-plate spring
33. Sear nose
34. Rear guard screw

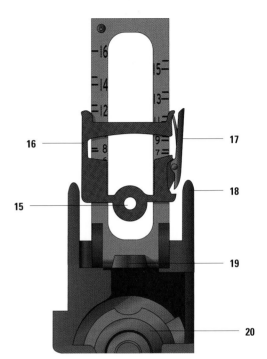

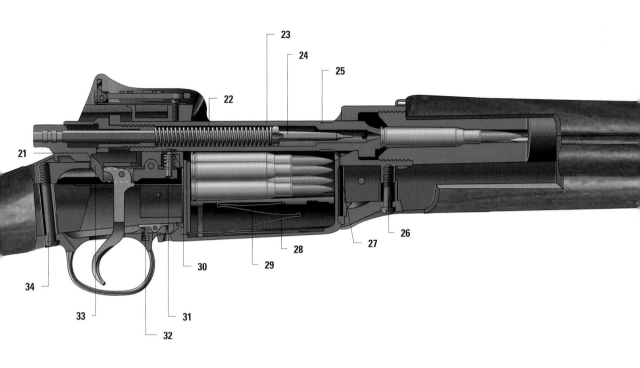

The Model 1917 rifle

By early 1915, manufacture of the British P14 rifle had also been contracted to three companies in the United States: Winchester Repeating Arms Company, Remington Arms Company and the Eddystone Manufacturing Company. For service with US forces the P14 was rechambered for the .30-06 Springfield round, and was designated the United States Rifle, cal. .30, Model of 1917. By the end of World War I, the Model 1917 rifle – the 'American Enfield' – had actually been manufactured in larger numbers than the Springfield Model 1903.

Although never issued with a telescopic sight, the Model 1917 rifle was used to great effect by many American sharpshooters, possibly the most famous example being provided by a US Army soldier who was not a trained sniper. While on patrol on 8 October 1918, Sergeant Alvin C. York of the 328th Infantry Regiment engaged a machine-gun unit with his Model 1917 rifle, killing 18 Germans with 18 shots (and a further nine with a pistol) and capturing 132 others, for which he was deservedly awarded the Congressional Medal of Honor.

An interesting photo of an American sniper using a scoped SMLE rifle. There were insufficient Springfield Model 1903 sniping rifles supplied in the early months following the United States' entry to World War I, and many American snipers who had trained with SMLEs continued to use them until sufficient quantities of Model 1903s became available. (US Army)

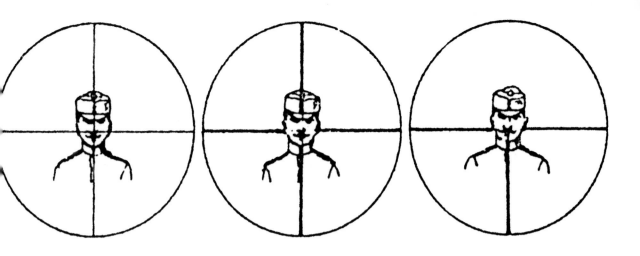

USE
Snipers in action

Developing the rifles and telescopes for sniping was all very well, but the fundamental challenge confronting all of the armies that required snipers was to ensure that they possessed not only the right mental attitude and capabilities, but also that their training was the best that could possibly be provided.

A diagram from a rare German sniper manual, showing how to zero three different patterns of reticles. All use the teeth of the target as the point of aim.

SNIPER SELECTION AND TRAINING

Germany

From the beginning of World War I sniping formed a fundamental part of German military strategy, so it is important to emphasize the sheer scale of the requirement the German Army had for trained snipers. Pre-war training manuals specified that a line-infantry regiment should field between 24 and 36 snipers at any given time, although this number could and did vary considerably. If one assumes an average of 30 snipers were fielded per day by a single battalion on a front of 25 miles, which was approximately the total length of the Somme front, then there could be up to 5,130 snipers operating, or approximately one for every 80yd of the line.

Unlike the British Army and its Dominion allies, in which by late 1915 all snipers were volunteers, the armies of the Central Powers selected their men on the basis of good marksmanship, the ability to keep a steady nerve under fire, or because they had specifically requested sniper duty. Mannfried Gossen was 18 years old when he volunteered as a sniper. He had always been a natural shot, and after watching a sniper working in his trench, he asked if he could try the rifle. Very shortly Gossen had his first kill and as a result was selected for sniper training.

A German sniper and observer shooting from a loophole set in a parapet in 1914 or 1915. The neatness of the sandbags was a disadvantage and later the Germans would deliberately construct parapets that were multi-coloured and covered in rubbish. Until the summer of 1916, German soldiers did not have steel helmets, so most snipers wore the soft *Feldmütze* cap.

Possessing good technology is one thing, but being trained sufficiently well enough to make proper and effective use of that technology was quite another; unlike many armies in August 1914, the German Army had recognized this requirement and provided its *Scharfschützen* with scheduled training.

Initially, in the German Army, there was no tuition provided at all for other ranks. Only NCOs were given sniper training, at one of several infantry training schools in Prussia, Bavaria, Saxony and elsewhere. Successful NCOs were returned to the front and required to disseminate what they had learned to their men, but it was a method that did not always work efficiently in practice. The NCOs were also in charge of the scoped rifles that were issued to men who met the requirements for sniping. This methodology ignored the fact that some NCOs were excellent snipers but had little or no ability to teach what they had learned, while others knew the theory inside out, but were not good front-line snipers in practice.

At first, the teaching was rigid in structure and followed the military doctrine of the pre-war period, which was based upon the precepts of open warfare. By the end of 1916, however, analysis of the lessons learned during more than two years of trench warfare made it clear that German sniper training was outmoded, ignored the real requirements of day-to-day trench sniping and needed to be improved, so additional training schools were established behind the lines. Details of these are very sketchy, but Metz, Saint-Quentin, Lille and Bapaume all had facilities and there were doubtless many others. Neophyte snipers were trained by combat-experienced sniper NCOs on a basic 10–14-day course that covered rifle handling and shooting, telescopic sight use, adjustment and maintenance, camouflage, observation and fieldcraft. The training had its weak points, however; for example, until the end of the war German snipers were instructed in the use of high vantage points such as church towers, windmills and treetops – places that the Allies considered death-traps for a sniper. Nor was cooperation between pairs of men (one observing, one shooting) considered mandatory, and as a consequence many German snipers worked alone.

Austria–Hungary

Austro-Hungarian snipers were trained along near-identical lines to those of the German Army, but with the addition of a specialist winter sniper training school established in the Seetal Alps between Scheifling and Zeltweg. Only there was it possible for snipers to learn how to contend with the unique conditions of mountain sniping. Much of the training given to ordinary infantry snipers was of limited use; specialist camouflage was hardly required (white was naturally predominant) and unlike an ordinary sniper, a mountain sniper could not expect to take up a position in a hide for more than a couple of hours as the numbing cold gradually froze the body. Training was also more complex. As well as receiving instruction in ordinary ground-based sniping, trainee mountain snipers learned to cope not only with high open vistas and long-range shooting but also, in a strange paradox, with close-range shooting in places where the trenches and other field positions could literally be overlooked by those of the enemy. Range instruction was also different, for with the high open vistas long-range shooting was possible in a manner that was inconceivable in the confines of ground-level trench warfare.

ABOVE LEFT
An early-war photograph of a German sniper showing the leather carry-case for his scope. He is wearing the minimum equipment he would require for trench sniping.

ABOVE RIGHT
A pair of Austrians. The sniper (at right) holds his scoped M95 rifle and a pair of binoculars. His companion has a M95 carbine, its use indicating that the Austrians are quite close to the Italian lines. Note the heavy cleated climbing boots.

The British Empire

Initially, good shots were selected: Private Thomas O. Durst of The King's Royal Rifle Corps had been a pre-war target shooter and had qualified as a marksman on the British Army ranges. On his arrival in France he was 'volunteered' by his sergeant for sniper training. He was ordered to go to a new training school, although he was not entirely sure what was involved, and had to find his own way there. Luckily he met up with a few other neophyte snipers who were in the same situation, and they agreed that whatever happened, they were fortunate to be out of the front lines for a while.

It soon became evident, however, that although many of these men were good shots, they simply did not necessarily possess the right mental or physical attributes. After all, shooting someone in the head from 200yd with the aid of a telescopic sight was an entirely different matter from the more leisurely pastime of hitting a static bull's-eye on a range, as Major Eric Penberthy, a Canadian later to become commander of the Third Army School of Scouting, Observation and Sniping, noted (Penberthy 1920: 67).

The selection of men with the right temperament for the job was vital, in part because of the time, cost and effort required to train them, but also because subsequent failure on their part to do their job properly reflected badly on the sniping courses and could ultimately lead to unnecessary deaths. All too often troublemakers, slackers or the hopelessly inept were sent for sniper training as a means of getting them out of the hair of their officers (Freemantle 1916: 87). The problem was that company commanders wanted to hang on to the good men, so there was a general tendency to 'volunteer' the inept, undisciplined or lazy – which made life difficult for the instructors and the sniping companies.

Major Nevill A.D. Armstrong, who later went on to help command the hugely successful Canadian Corps School of Sniping, has been frequently quoted for his observations about the best type of recruits being hunters, woodsmen and others at home in the outdoors (Armstrong 1942: 3). Although Armstrong was primarily referring to those who proved successful in the Canadian Army, his comments are an accurate assessment of the self-reliant types who were best suited to sniping. Although hunters and trappers were few and far between in the British Army, there were many men who possessed the right attitude; the problem was in finding them. The psychology of sniping was not understood at the time and it required men who could mentally detach themselves when they worked (today it is referred to as 'being in the bubble'), regarding their job as necessary, but not personal. The desire to attain good shooting, a clean kill and a job well done was the paramount motivation. Many could not do this and no sniper the author has ever interviewed from any time period has expressed any pleasure in killing. Sergeant Thomas E. Randal, a British volunteer serving as a sniper with the 82nd (Calgary) Battalion CEF, wrote candidly from Vimy in April 1917 that although he had had plenty of shooting, he took no pleasure in killing and tried his best to forget how many times he had shot a German, despite his enthusiasm for sniping.

Fortunately, the British Army had a few senior officers who believed passionately in the efficacy of sniping, and they had a champion in Major Hesketh V. Hesketh-Prichard. His attempts to enlist in a British Army line regiment had failed, but in March 1915 he was finally accepted into the Intelligence Corps as officer in charge of war correspondents. While escorting the newspapermen around the lines he was horrified by the amount of sniping emanating from the German lines and the lack of response from the British, noting that no one dared show their head because the whole German line was in full sight (Hesketh-Prichard 1994: 33). He began to take with him his own scoped hunting rifles and whenever he had the chance, he used them to indulge in a quite unofficial sniping war. Questioning line officers and the few available snipers made him realize that their knowledge of sniping was almost non-existent and that there was an urgent necessity for some form of organized training to be introduced. The encounter he recorded with a bewildered private in late 1915 was typical (Hesketh-Prichard 1994: 43). When he asked if the man had actually shot the scoped rifle he was holding, the answer was no. He asked if the man had been trained to use it. Again the answer was no. When he enquired how it had been issued to him, the answer was simply that it was trench stores.

Hesketh-Prichard was heartened, however, by the number of individual regiments he came across that were at least making an effort to take on the might of the German *Scharfschützen*. The method of snapshooting over the sandbag parapet, so often used in the fighting at Gallipoli (see pages 59 and 62), did not work well on the Western Front against a skilled enemy armed with optically equipped rifles. Two seconds' exposure was long enough to receive a retaliatory bullet in the head. He observed that there was nothing in the way of trench material to help snipers and despaired of the obsessive neatness of the British trenches, noting that because the sandbag parapets had been neatly beaten down with spades, it meant that a mouse couldn't move along them without being spotted (Hesketh-Prichard 1994: 50).

Trainee snipers from The King's Royal Rifle Corps and The Rifle Brigade at the sniping school at Acq in northern France, early 1916. The legend behind reads 'The Snipers' Panopticum'. A panopticon was an optical instrument that combined elements of a telescope and microscope.

Hesketh-Prichard's ability, enthusiasm and apparently limitless energy impressed officers and men alike, and it became obvious in the sectors where he was working that effective counter-sniping had a serious effect on the Germans, who quickly became far more cautious. With the tacit approval of some senior officers, in September 1915 he was eventually released from his employment at GHQ and attached as sniping officer for the Third Army.

While the importance of Hesketh-Prichard's pioneering work cannot be underestimated, it should be stressed that the British Army was not entirely oblivious to the need for trained snipers. While the School of Musketry at Hythe in Kent was doing its best to train officers and senior NCOs, it could not meet the requirements for instructing large numbers of men, so a new branch was established in 1914 at Bisley Camp in Surrey under the command of Major Thomas F. Freemantle. In typically parsimonious fashion the British Army would not sanction the provision of training ammunition for the school, which had to purchase supplies from Fulton's Ltd of Bisley, or 'borrow' unattended stocks from British Army units training on the ranges. So successful did the training schedule prove, however, that in spring 1916 Freemantle was promoted to lieutenant-colonel and placed in charge of a new Northern Command School of Scouting and Sniping at Rugeley in Staffordshire.

Meanwhile, Hesketh-Prichard was gaining support through personal sniping demonstrations as he and his second-in-command, Lieutenant Geoffrey M. Gathorne-Hardy, undertook countless exhausting instructional tours of the lines, and in January 1916 he was finally granted permission to establish a sniping school in Béthune in northern France. By July 1916 the school was self-supporting and Hesketh-Prichard was instructed to proceed to First Army HQ and establish the First Army School of Scouting, Observation and Sniping in a small village called Linghem, near the town of Aire in north-eastern France. Linghem was usefully sited at the foot of a large plateau and this choice of location enabled a range of 1,000yd to be established, the first of its type in France. Finally, it seemed sniping was going to become an officially recognized British Army skill.

The instructional course set up was long, at 17 days, but covered in great detail the rifles (both the SMLE and P14), telescopic sights and their function, the Scout telescope, map reading and use of the marching compass, ground and cover, camouflage and its special applications, stalking and scouting, establishing sniping posts, front-line observation and reporting, sketching and deciphering aerial reconnaissance photographs. According to lecture notes made by Lieutenant F.I. Ford of 1st Battalion, The Leicestershire Regiment, handed out at the Second Army School of Scouting, Observation and Sniping at Acq in northern France, the objective of sniping was fourfold: to damage enemy morale; to inflict casualties on the enemy; to hinder his activities; and to strike back against his snipers.

All of the training was of course interspersed with much shooting practice utilizing telescopic and iron sights, at all ranges up to 1,000yd. The training was so thorough that with little modification it still forms the basis not only for British sniper training, but also for that of many other

A sniper training range, with British instructors and Australian riflemen, shooting without telescopic sights. The officer left of centre, happily clutching the muzzle of his rifle, has a German Zeiss prismatic scope on his weapon. (© IWM CO 35)

countries as well. At the end of the training course, there was an examination with a pass requirement of 70 per cent.

The First Army sniping school was aided by a casual visit to Linghem by Simon C.J. Joseph, the 16th Lord Lovat, in the autumn of 1916. He had been greatly impressed by Hesketh-Prichard's unique use of the General Service and Scout Regiment telescopes, powerful 22× or 20× three-draw brass-bodied instruments used by Highland ghillies. These powerful instruments were difficult to use properly and Hesketh-Prichard needed help in finding men who were experienced in the use of them. The Lovat Scouts' ranks were full of just such men who spent their lives stalking deer and were perfectly suited for the job. The Lovat Sharpshooters had only been formed in October of that year but the 200 volunteers were clearly insufficient in number to provide an effective sniping force. Instead, Lord Lovat discussed with Hesketh-Prichard the possibility of using the Lovat Sharpshooters in a training role and so the focus of their employment was changed. Henceforth they would become observers or 'glassmen' rather than snipers, to help train the pupils at the sniping schools that were being rapidly established. They also provided the snipers with a vital item of clothing, still in use today: the ghillie suit.

A Canadian Divisional Sniper Training School was set up at Shorncliffe in Kent in October 1915 and from the outset the Canadian training was conducted along slightly different lines from that of the British. The syllabus was different, with only 40 officers and men per course, equally divided, and it was only 14 days in length.

When the Allied army was eventually withdrawn from Gallipoli in early 1916, Australian and New Zealand Army Corps (ANZAC) snipers redeployed to the Western Front were sent to be trained at one of the British Army sniping schools, an experience they found interesting, but challenging. Many ANZAC snipers did not take to telescopic sights easily, and the discipline of obeying training schedules and keeping copious intelligence notes was alien to them. What they really excelled in was the mobile fighting of 1918.

France

Although almost nothing survives today of the training regimes, if any, employed for French snipers, it is more than possible that selected marksmen were issued with some of the few scoped rifles available. There are no accounts of French soldiers being trained under British auspices, so learning how to survive as a French Army sniper in the front line may well have been taught through attachment to an already-experienced sniper, in the same manner that the Germans initially employed.

French sniping at Verdun appears to have been minimal, as combat ranges were normally so close that grenades and pistols were of more practical use. Moreover, the tangled and heavily wooded terrain was initially difficult for snipers; it was only later in the fighting, when the hills had been turned into a shell-blasted lunar landscape, that trench sniping became the norm, the slightest exposure drawing fire.

Italy

Some details have been published over the years concerning the specific use of Italian Army snipers to eliminate enemy forward observers, who were regarded as a priority target. A corps famous for their marksmanship, the Bersaglieri (on a par with British Rifle regiments and German *Jäger* units), appear to have had a selection and training system for their snipers and this cannot have been unique among Italian Army regiments. Ottavio Bottecchia, the winner of the 1924 Tour de France and the first Italian to win that prestigious competition, was one of the Italian Army's highest-scoring snipers; he served in a Bersaglieri regiment on the Alpine Front.

It is not known how well the Filotecnica scope performed and the number of Carcano rifles so equipped remains unclear, but in all probability only a few hundred ever saw service.

An American sniper holds up his Springfield Model 1903 sniping rifle for the camera. It has the ubiquitous Warner & Swasey M1913 sight, and has been painted with two or three colours for camouflage effect – something rarely encountered in images of British sniping rifles. (US Army)

The United States

The US armed forces were utterly unprepared for any major conflict when the United States declared war on Germany on 6 April 1917. The US Army had a strength of 100,000 men, augmented by 112,000 National Guardsmen (fewer than the British Expeditionary Force in 1914), with not a single sniper among them. There was no doubt in the minds of the Army's leadership that sniper training was required, but how to do it posed a real problem as there were no US Army instructors. Fortunately, the National Rifle Association, based at Camp Perry, Ohio, contained the crème de la crème of American competitive shooters: J.H. Keough, W.A. Libbey, M.C. Momma and W.H. Richard were just a few of the instructors who had between them won almost every shooting prize available. Although not snipers, they provided a core of experienced and very enthusiastic instructors whose numbers were bolstered by the transfer of some British and Canadian sniper instructors, such as the Canadians H.W. McBride, F. Crossland and J.A. McKenzie and the Britons S. Grey, A.R. Hall and J.W. Right.

This massing of shooting talent boded well for US Army recruits, who rotated through Camp Perry on an exhaustive 30-day course, 22 days of which included live-firing up to 1,000yd. The eclectic mix of American shooting instructors and British and Dominion combat-experienced snipers was well-nigh perfect, for each group possessed specialist skills augmented by the other. They imitated the British Army sniping schools in France by creating realistic front lines with trenches, ruined buildings and barbed wire. Papier-mâché heads of German soldiers were exposed at random and a sniper was expected to score a hit within two seconds at 200yd. Nor did the US Army lag behind when it came to inventive training, Major Simon W. Brookhart creating a new means of calculating ranges using 'milliradians' (now used today as 'mildot'), and range-finding

American snipers on a training exercise, wearing ghillie suits and head covering. Their rifles, with scopes dismounted, are well camouflaged with strips of sacking. (© IWM Q 65492)

charts were produced that enabled calculations to be made when shooting uphill or downhill – something not taught in sniper training until the 1980s. Even so, the training programme was insufficient to meet the US Army's sniper requirements, so American riflemen in France were seconded to attend the British and Canadian sniping schools at the front, at Linghem, Acq, Béthune and Vadencourt. As Hesketh-Prichard later wrote, when the Americans finally entered World War I, the British were delighted as they appeared to have an unlimited supply of competent men and good equipment (Hesketh-Prichard 1994: 91).

The US Marine Corps also had its share of problems. Commanded separately from the US Army, it boasted a long tradition of highly successful competitive shooting and decided to set up its own training centre at Marine Barracks, Quantico in Virginia, early in 1918 under the command of a Canadian officer, Major Arthur C. Sutton. Only Marines who had qualified as 'Expert Riflemen' were eligible to join the course, which taught a syllabus very similar to that of the Canadian Expeditionary Force, including very long-range shooting out to 1,200yd. Although this may seem at odds with the requirements of trench sniping, it should be remembered that by early 1918 the fighting had moved to open warfare. The trouble was that by the time both infantry and sniper training had been completed, a US Marine Corps recruit who trained at Quantico would be unlikely to be in France until very late in 1918, so exactly how many of the school's 450 qualified snipers ever served is unknown and the numbers of scoped sniping rifles available was extremely low. That said, there were certainly many Marines who gave a good account of themselves sniping with iron sights, in particular a cadre of Native Americans who, like their Canadian counterparts, exacted a heavy toll on the Germans, several being awarded the Congressional Medal of Honor as a result.

Two examples of snipers' insignia issued during World War I: at left, the German bronze oak leaves cap badge; at right, the British blackened brass scout/sniper fleur-de-lis sleeve badge, originally introduced during the Second Anglo-Boer War (1899–1902). Sniper insignia was virtually never worn in combat, as the summary execution of snipers of both sides was not unknown.

SNIPERS IN ACTION

To be a front-line sniper was no sinecure. True, snipers were excused wearying fatigues and sentry duties and among the front-line soldiers they were probably the only ones who might possibly get sufficient sleep when on a tour of trench duty; but their casualty rates were in excess of 50 per cent, as dealing with an equally experienced enemy meant that just one small error – the light glinting from a scope lens, a slight involuntary movement, poor choice of camouflage or positioning – invariably meant that there was no second chance.

Sniping in the opening battles

The employment of German and Austrian snipers in the first months of World War I was mostly on an ad hoc basis. In mobile warfare, the greatest threat to German Army forces operating in Belgium and France was understood to come not from well-concealed enemy snipers, as hardly any existed, but from *franc-tireurs* (free-shooters), concealed marksmen who were often civilians; savage reprisals were inflicted on civilian populations as a result. The reality was that much of the shooting that targeted German troops was not sniping as such, but fire from concealed Belgian Army or French Army riflemen.

Nevertheless, in the fluid fighting of 1914 it was remarkably straightforward for German snipers to target senior enemy officers, for German marksmen could easily infiltrate Allied lines. Some idea of their effectiveness can be gauged from the fact that by the end of 1914, ten British generals had been shot dead, their deaths even credited by the British press to 'enemy snipers'. With the gradual establishment of trench systems in the winter of 1914, sniping settled down into more of a routine, and all sides became far more cautious; this period saw the birth of the techniques of trench sniping, counter-sniping, concealment and observation that would eventually coalesce into the methods used to teach neophyte snipers up to the present day.

Commercial sporting rifles played a vital part in providing the German Army with the wherewithal to assert its sniping superiority in the first year of World War I and they deserve some recognition, although little has

been written about them. The collection and distribution of these commercial rifles was organized under the auspices of a high-ranking German Army officer, Victor II the Duke of Ratibor. As Germany was preparing for war in early 1914, the call went out to all patriotic Germans who possessed good, optically equipped hunting rifles to hand them over to the German Army for the duration of the conflict; for those who were reluctant, this request was backed up by law. From the start of 1915 it became an offence to own an undeclared sporting rifle and the mayors of local communities were instructed to ensure all such weapons were handed over.

There has long been a question mark over exactly how many commercial rifles were provided to the German Army prior to the outbreak of World War I. Hesketh-Prichard estimated that some 20,000 were in German military hands by December 1914, but this figure may have included some of the newly introduced Gew 98 sniping rifles. A more conservative estimate is that perhaps between 8,000 and 10,000 commercial rifles were supplied, which if true, was still between 8,000 and 10,000 more than the British Army possessed. That they were used to good effect was obvious, for accounts of the heavy fighting of 1914 are littered with references to the effectiveness of German snipers. For example, an unnamed soldier of 1st Battalion, The Royal Irish Fusiliers noted that his battalion had advanced into Armentières in September 1914 but continued to suffer at the hands of German snipers. The house in which the British soldiers were resting was regularly peppered with bullets, causing many casualties, including one unwary Irishman who was shot through the head (Moreno & Truedale 2004: 26).

It is of course impossible to determine whether these German riflemen were simply marksmen using standard rifles, or snipers equipped with scoped rifles, but from later comments about accurate shooting at dusk and dawn, when a scope was particularly efficient, it would seem to indicate the latter. Because of their light construction and thin barrels, these rifles were susceptible to accidental damage and it was imperative that sufficient numbers of scoped Gew 98 sniping rifles were issued as quickly as possible.

One unconsidered side-effect for the British, using large-calibre hunting rifles in response, was that if sniping, such weapons had to be fired from a standing position, not prone, as sniping officer Lieutenant Stuart Cloete recalled (Cloete 1972: 74). He used a .600 Express sporting rifle very effectively to stove in a German sniper plate. Such was the weapon's recoil, however, that it could only be shot from a standing position.

Sniping in the trenches

Between the end of 1914 and March 1918, sniping remained primarily a specialized form of trench warfare. Snipers were regarded as of little practical

This French sniper serving at Verdun is armed with the Lebel/ APX combination. To the sniper's right there is a hide, so he has been posed for the benefit of the photographer. (Laurence Brown)

use during trench raids or on patrols, and were predominantly employed as observers, tackling enemy snipers or looking for targets of opportunity.

As the opening battles gave way to a static war in the trenches, German snipers on the Western Front began to be issued with the new SmK armour-piercing ammunition. An SmK bullet exited from the muzzle of a rifle with a pressure behind it of a little over 18 tons per square inch and a German technical paper produced in March 1915 stated that tests with SmK bullets showed it to have an impressive performance, capable of penetrating 11mm (almost 0.5in) of high-quality chrome-nickel steel plate at a distance of 100m (109yd) if the plate stood vertically and if it was set at 60°, 6mm (almost 0.25in).

For the unofficial British and Dominion sniper sections that had gradually been formed in the front lines of the Western Front in early months of 1915, the first priority was to create an environment from where they were able to view the enemy and be able to respond to their sniping by whatever means were at their disposal – preferably without putting their own lives in unnecessary danger. This was easier said than done, however, for they were hampered by a total lack of suitable equipment; no scoped rifles or sniper plates were available and whatever was needed was usually hastily improvised on site. At this early stage in the war, Britain had virtually no protective plate for sniping use and what was available was often borrowed scraps of mild steel that were barely able to stop an ordinary round of ball ammunition. Corporal William Skipp recalled just such a makeshift sniper position, featuring a sheet of metal 2in high and 12in wide with an aperture for a rifle barrel (Arthur 2002: 87).

As Major Armstrong, former Bisley competitor and himself a sniping officer, noted, unorganized sniping was ineffectual; the absence of proper direction meant that snipers were lacking in guidance, instruction, discipline and focus (Armstrong 1942: 22). Officially, and perhaps indicating exactly what Army Command thought of the importance of sniping in general, in the British Army the strength of a battalion sniping section was fixed at a mere eight men, plus an officer, sergeant and corporal in charge. (This compared to 30 in the German Army.) The second lieutenant in charge was originally termed the Sniping Officer, but later became the Intelligence and Sniping Officer, as it became increasingly vital to be able to interpret the men's observations clearly and send reports to the brigade intelligence HQ. According to sniping instructor Major Frederick M. Crum, a battalion sniping establishment should consist of a minimum of 16 men plus officer, sergeant and corporal, but he added that sometimes 24 men or more might be required, and a list of suitable men was kept on hand by the sniping sergeant (Crum 1921: 21).

In practice the number of men actually selected by their battalion for sniping could and did vary hugely and depended entirely on the attitude of the lieutenant-colonel commanding. Some, such as 1/5th Battalion, The Hampshire Regiment, had only ten men in their sniper section at first, but the history of 1/15th (County of London) Battalion (Prince of Wales's Own Civil Service Rifles), The London Regiment, recorded that in June 1916 the unit's sniping section was 30 strong, which was 3 per cent of the total of the battalion's manpower and that they were made up of civil servants, clerks, merchants, commercial travellers, engineers, gardeners, waiters – in fact just about every civilian profession one could imagine. The casualty rates were high though, with some 50 per cent being killed or wounded (Knight 2004: 67).

Unlike the German Army, there was a distinction in the British Army between being a company and battalion sniper, although it was largely one of location. A battalion sniper was free to move anywhere along the battalion front, working wherever he believed was best, or at the specific request of a company or platoon that was experiencing localized problems. Company snipers tended to be more static, occupying posts

Although often reproduced, this is a good image of a working pair of German snipers somewhere on the Verdun front in 1916. The sniper has his scope carry-case and fighting knife (far more useful than a bayonet). Curiously, Mauser sniping rifles had polished bolts and the gleam from this is clearly visible in this picture.

A Scout Regiment three-draw telescope on a late-war tripod. Although tiring to use, these heavy instruments were extremely powerful. A good 'glassman' could see troop movements clearly at 5 miles' distance.

SNIPER DRESS AND EQUIPMENT

What the sniper wore was dependent on his position in the line. According to British sniping instructors, a well-concealed sniper should be invisible to an observer at 20yd. Men working from trench hides or ruined buildings were well concealed and usually had little more than basic service dress, along with ammunition, water and the tools of their trade. If working from a sap (a narrow deep trench dug into no man's land) then he required minimal camouflage composed of local vegetation, usually in the form of a concealing headdress such as a sandbag or suitable piece of

netting over the head and face. The most dangerous positions were in no man's land itself, where careful body camouflage was a necessity and dummies such as dead trees, cows, horses or even fake corpses were often used.

If lying in open country, Allied snipers wore camouflaged suits. The ghillie suit took several forms, but was basically a loose-fitting burlap or cloth coat, reaching to below the knee, with a belt, a hood incorporating eye-holes or a fine-mesh veil, and long open sleeves. It was covered in ragged strips of coloured sacking, often

The *Stirnpanzer* armoured brow plate, the only item of trench armour practical for a sniper to wear, although its weight had a tendency to tip the steel helmet down over the shooter's eyes.

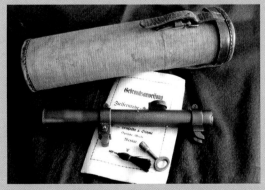

A German Goerz scope with its issue carry-case, instruction manual, adjuster key and lens brush. This short variant was the basis for the series of British Aldis-pattern scopes.

A pair of British Army-issue sniper's binoculars, made by Jumelles of Paris; they are 3× with very basic focal adjustment. Frustratingly, although named to 'Cpl. S. Baker, D Coy Snipers', no regiment is given.

A British sniper wearing the simplest of camouflage, a sandbag hood. It was perfectly adequate for sniping from a concealed hide or sap as long as the sniper was well dug in. (© IWM Q 95962)

painted in shades of green, brown and black, rendering it usefully shapeless. Ghillie suits have now become an all-encompassing expression, but Symien suits, devised by Royal Engineers officer Lieutenant Lindsay .D. Symington, were also produced in very large numbers. Unlike the burlap or cloth ghillie suit, the Symien suit was made of khaki canvas and could be a robe or top and trousers, painted as required. It was not shapeless and relied on careful colouring to blend with the surrounding vegetation.

While speed and accuracy of shooting were emphasized during German Army sniper training, there was not as much importance placed on camouflage and observation; camouflaged suits were not commonly employed, for example. It is often asserted that German snipers wore the cumbersome body armour introduced in spring 1917, but this is quite erroneous. The four-piece suit of armour was designed for use in exposed locations by static troops such as sentries and machine-gunners. It was immensely heavy at about 22lb, uncomfortable to wear for any length of time and crucially had no provision for a rifle to be held to the shoulder to fire it. (The author has tried it, and it is impossible). Moreover, most snipers lay down to shoot, rendering the suit utterly pointless. The only piece of this ensemble that there is photographic evidence for sniper use was the *Stirnpanzer* armoured brow plate. Although the *Stirnpanzer* weighed a hefty 4.4lb, when mounted on the front of the steel helmet it could provide protection from rifle bullet fired from 50yd.

within their company frontage and primarily counter-sniping or working to very specific instructions.

That the British Army's sniper training was paying off began to show, for where its snipers were actively working, the level of British casualties dropped dramatically. In places, the Germans were so stunned at the retribution being inflicted upon them, that they all but ceased sniping. Manfried Gossen spoke of the change this brought about, commenting that his unit was faced by a Welsh battalion with some excellent snipers. Gossen was lucky to escape with his life when one put a bullet through his cap as he was observing with his binoculars. This fortuitously put Gossen out of action for much of the Somme battle.

In some places, the level of German sniping dropped to the comical by the end of 1915. When a Scottish sniper was seen walking down a trench with a brace of pheasants, he was asked where he had been. He explained he had been in no man's land stalking them but he was in no danger, as the Germans dare not show themselves in daylight anymore.

The Canadian Expeditionary Force (CEF) policy on sniping was uncompromising, combining aggression and dominance. They believed, with some justification, that three-man sniper teams were better than two, with one man detailed as sniper, a second as observer and the third aiding in either capacity to allow the others to rest their eyes, as observing was an extremely tiring occupation despite the fact that all were sniper trained.

From early 1915 Canadian troops began to man the front lines on the Western Front. The CEF was extremely fortunate in having within its ranks many hunters and trappers plus a significant number of First Nation Canadians and they took to despatching their opposite numbers with highly professional competence. Henry Northwestwind (usually abbreviated to Norwest) of the 50th (Calgary) Battalion CEF was a Metis hunter and trapper, who believed it was his sacred duty to fulfil his destiny as a sniper; his official tally prior to his death on 18 August 1918 was 119.

The Canadians soon established themselves as a force to be reckoned with, believing the only possible policy for sniping was to utterly dominate the Germans and to establish total control over no man's land. Gossen later wrote that his unit had the Canadians in front of them, resulting in an almost total cessation of sniping from the German lines. The Canadians also believed in making use of their snipers on the offensive, in organized sections to cover advancing troops by targeting machine-gun positions, enemy snipers and observers – tactics later also adopted by the British. By the end of the war, the Canadians proved to have been the most successful of all the Dominion sniping contingents.

The British experience on the Somme in 1916 was pivotal in altering concepts of how snipers should be employed. German snipers were so effective that Lieutenant-Colonel Graham Seton Hutchinson, a Machine Gun Corps officer, commented that his guns, sited near High Wood, had to be repositioned so that they could no longer be seen by the Germans, as the fire from their snipers at long range (over 600yd) was proving too accurate to be comfortable. Ten brigadier-generals were killed by

German snipers during the battle and on 1 July 1916 it is believed that 11 British battalion commanders fell victim to aimed sniper fire. Counter-sniping was urgently needed, but many of the trained British snipers, serving as ordinary infantry, had been killed in the advance.

A sniper section of The Queen's (Royal West Surrey Regiment) in France. Note the wide variation in the ages of the snipers. All three rifles are SMLEs; the weapon at left is fitted with a PPCo scope, the rifle at right with an Aldis scope in Purdey mounts. (Stephen J. Chambers)

Snipers on the Somme, 1916 (overleaf)

By the end of 1915 the British had started to employ their snipers in a more offensive manner, and German snipers were no longer able to claim unchallenged dominance of the battlefield. Here we see a British sniper, of the 10th Lincolns in the 34th Division wearing a home-made camouflaged head covering, working with his spotter from a concealed position on the edge of a wheatfield. He is using the relatively rare combination of an SMLE Mk III rifle and Winchester A5 telescopic sight. Although fewer than 1,000 of this combination were produced, it was claimed by many snipers to have been the most effective British rifle-and-scope combination of World War I. Unlike the Germans, British snipers worked in pairs and the spotter was invariably a trained sniper as well. Here he is using the powerful 20× General Service Mk IV Signallers telescope, which was unique among the combatant forces; every other country issued binoculars to snipers.

The German sniper, working alone and hidden inside the cover of a ruined cottage, is wearing little in the way of camouflage, just his issue Pattern 1907/10 tunic, but has the newly issued Modell 1916 *Stahlhelm*, which could provide protection against a long-range rifle bullet or shrapnel balls. His rifle is the ubiquitous Gew 98 with a 3× Zeiss scope. German snipers were well trained to use natural cover and did not resort to camouflage clothing as much as their Allied counterparts. Unlike Britain, with limited resources for optical manufacture, Germany had innumerable types of sniping rifle available, including many commercial patterns produced for hunting.

A SNIPER'S DAY

Snipers would crawl to their positions in the darkness before dawn, either a trench dugout or on the battlefield in a prepared hide, and they would remain there during daylight hours. If snipers were spotted, it would result in retaliatory artillery fire, so they needed a quick exit to a trench or other place of safety. Whenever possible, a sniper tried to ensure at least two exits were available to him. Static positions between the trenches were dangerous in the extreme, for a sniper rarely had an easy means of escape if spotted, and shots taken were normally very sparing indeed. More often, such open positions became used as much for intelligence gathering as sniping.

The period at dawn and dusk became known as 'sniper's light' – a slightly surreal twilight world where nothing could be discerned clearly with the naked eye. Some snipers were, of course, equipped with light-magnifying telescopic sights, which enabled them to see and shoot the unwary or the careless who believed that they were somehow invisible. Those times of day were also normally windless, making long-range shooting possible, providing the light was sufficient. Dusk was also a fruitful time, when ordinary soldiers began to relax, cook and smoke, and the latter was probably responsible for more deaths than any other single factor. Smoke could be smelt and also seen against the sky, and the old warning of bad luck following the lighting of three cigarettes from one match was based on fact. The flare of a match (clearly visible from 1,000yd) alerted the sniper, lighting the second cigarette gave him time to settle his aim, and the third smoker would usually be the unlucky target. Such acuity of vision was not exceptional by any means – one British officer on night patrol commented on the number of near-misses and was told sharply to remove his luminous wristwatch, as the sniper could see it.

By nightfall, the sniper, usually cramped, tired, hungry and with eyes red from strain would make his way back to his lines and send his report in. He may not have fired a shot, but if he was simply observing, it might contain vital information about machine-gun or artillery emplacements, or perhaps troop movements.

The Royal Engineers' Special Works section was responsible for many ingenious devices to aid snipers. Here a dummy German corpse has been made. The sniper would use a deep covered sap to reach it, and with care could use it several times before it became too dangerous to do so. (© IWM Q 95960)

A British sniper sergeant, wearing a sniper veil and leather face-mask with protective goggles. The mask would prevent the condensation from his cold breath from giving his position away, and help prevent misting of the scope. The goggles were worn predominantly for training purposes, with dark lenses to simulate night-time operations, but would hardly ever be used in the field. (Lawrence Brown)

A British line-battalion sniper's position built into a trench. The sniper leaving has pulled back the heavy canvas 'door'. No-one was allowed in or out until permission was granted, as the position of an open loophole could be given away by the sudden flash of light behind it, created by the curtain being opened. (© IWM Q 8454)

A sniper section of the 21st (Eastern Ontario) Battalion CEF. At far left is Corporal Johnson Paudash, an Ojibwa who had 88 confirmed kills. All the rifles are Ross M1910s with Warner & Swasey sights. Note that the front woodwork of the Ross rifles has been removed to relieve pressure on the barrels – a modification forbidden on British Army sniping rifles.

The appalling waste of sniping skill and opportunity on the Somme was belatedly acknowledged by the British Army as it prepared for the attempted breakthrough battles of 1917. Prior to the battle of Messines (7–14 July 1917), ANZAC sniper teams tackled the many German pillboxes that posed a serious obstacle to the Allied advance. This they did with great success, forcing the German machine-gunners from their positions atop the bunkers and into cover inside, from where their fire was less effective; they also directed rifle fire through the loopholes, enabling teams armed with grenades to advance onto the enemy positions – tactics first used by the Germans at Verdun.

The actions immediately before the Third Battle of Ypres (31 July–10 November 1917) saw Allied snipers being detailed to support the advance by moving along the front and flanks to deal with any significant opposition. As a result, one of only two Victoria Crosses awarded to snipers during World War I was won by 22-year-old Private Thomas Barratt of 7th Battalion, The South Staffordshire Regiment, on 27 July 1917. (The other VC was won by Lance-Corporal John Thomas of 2/5th Battalion, The Prince of Wales's (North Staffordshire Regiment), on 30 November 1917.) Operating as a scout, Barratt moved towards the German line, his patrol receiving continuous fire from enemy snipers; Barratt stalked and killed his opposite numbers before covering the retirement of the patrol with his fire, thereby successfully holding off the Germans. Barratt survived these encounters and regained the British lines, only to be killed by an artillery shell.

Sniping beyond the Western Front

Aspects of sniping beyond the Western Front are almost impossible to determine, as little written documentary evidence in English exists. In those regions with open spaces, such as the Italian mountains, vast Russian wheatfields or deserts of the Near East, visibility was such that sniping at ration or work parties was possible at ranges that were simply impossible on the Western Front. As to how effective it was is impossible to know, however, but simply being under aimed fire would have prevented many routine and necessary tasks from being completed.

The sniping war at Gallipoli is often overlooked, for it was a remote and comparatively brief campaign (April 1915–January 1916) and there were virtually no telescopic-sighted rifles employed. Yet it was an extremely important testing-ground in terms of establishing how sniping worked, providing both the Ottoman and Allied armies with invaluable practical experience and helping the Allies to develop techniques that were later to be used on the Western Front.

Many of the Australian and New Zealand volunteers whose landed at Gallipoli in April 1915 believed at first that they were more fortunate than their comrades fighting through the rain and mud of the Western Front. While British soldiers faced the well-prepared and well-equipped German snipers in France and Flanders, the ANZAC troops landed in the Ottoman Army lines believing they were facing a conscript army with no enthusiasm for fighting and few military skills. They were soon soundly disabused of this, for not only was the Ottoman Army extremely competent, but within its ranks were a large number of excellent shots.

Although there were virtually no optically equipped rifles available to either side, at the short ranges that separated the trenches, this was no handicap. The ANZACs learned quickly, improvising methods of fighting the Turks, inventing useful tools such as periscope rifles, which used a pair of mirrors and a remotely mounted trigger on a wooden framework to give a view of the target. Snapshooting was very popular, with an observer calling as soon as a target was sighted allowing the sniper to bob up, fire and drop down in one movement. It took perfect teamwork and a detailed knowledge of the terrain in front to achieve results, but the ANZACs became very adept at it, although they could never claim to be able to beat the Turks at their own game.

There appeared to be no specific sniper training or issue of scoped rifles among the Ottoman Army forces at Gallipoli; instead, the Allied troops fighting in the Dardanelles campaign faced Turkish riflemen who had proved themselves to be expert shots, usually through years of game hunting. That many were extremely competent is not in doubt; several post-war Australian memoirs mention the uncanny accuracy of the Ottoman Army sharpshooters and enemy marksmen accounted for no fewer than five British and Australian and three French generals at Gallipoli.

The M1887 and M1888 Turkish Mausers' slightly smaller 7.65×53mm calibre proved perfectly adequate and sniping at Gallipoli was aided by two factors: the very efficient Turkish marksmen and the short ranges usually involved. The ANZAC forces that fought there were soon under

The Ulster/Neill sight was offset, allowing the iron sights to be used. The front sight required an aiming dot in its centre. (Dr R. Maze)

TESTING THE GALILEAN SIGHT

The Galilean sight's practicality has been brought into question over the years, but thanks to some very exhaustive field testing by Dr Robert Maze in 2011 and 2015 the type's effectiveness has become much clearer. Generally speaking, their performance was similar regardless of type. They provided a 2× or 2.5× magnification, but with a very reduced field of vision of between 1° and 1.5°. This equates in shooting terms to 5–7ft at a range of 100yd and meant any target that was moving above a snail's pace would quickly be out of the aim of the shooter, although their design meant that reverting to the rifle's iron sights was possible for shooters with quick reflexes.

The view through the Galilean sight was relatively dim due to the very small rear sight; and as the sight was not enclosed in a tube it meant that the shooter suffered from glare in bright sun,

The offset rear-aperture sight of the Ulster/Neill; it is affixed by using the retaining screw of the safety catch. (Dr R. Maze)

A Lattey front sight fitted to an SMLE rifle used at Gallipoli by Trooper Charles H. Livingstone of the 6th Light Horse Regiment AIF. (AWM REL 16524)

which could also cause the objective lens to flash, giving away the location of the shooter.

On the plus side, they were far cheaper to manufacture than a telescopic sight, had no complex internal parts, were mostly impervious to recoil or accidental damage, weighed virtually nothing and – most importantly – a rifle fitted with a Galilean sight could be fired through a loophole aperture because they were mounted overbore. Due to the optical properties of the Galilean lens system, they also provided a sharp target image out to about 1,500yd.

No accounts survive of the actual use of any Galilean-type sight for sniping, but what became apparent during recent testing was that the Gibbs, with its long sight radii and post and crosswire on the objective lens, performed better at longer ranges than the other simpler sights such as the Lattey and Martin. Under favourable conditions the shooters testing the Gibbs felt that it would be effective to around 300yd. Of course, in trench sniping where targets were seldom more than 200yd away and often much, much closer, there is no doubt that any of these Galilean sights would have provided the sniper with an enhanced target image that was more effective than those of SMLE rifle's iron sights. This is not to dismiss the standard iron sights as useless by any means, as was proven by many of the ANZAC snipers who used iron sights for sniping on Gallipoli. Most of them were kangaroo or deer hunters able to snapshoot out to 300yd.

The tiny rear sight for the Lattey, mounted to the standard iron rear sight. It provided a 2× magnified view of the target, and used the standard elevation latch. To provide a clear photograph, the rear-sight is set for about 1,200yd, roughly six times the Lattey's practical range. (AWM REL 16524)

During recent testing, the Gibbs was highly rated as the best of the Galilean sights. It has a front sight with red pointer and crosshair and uses a micro-adjustable Parker-Hale aperture rear sight. It clearly shows its target shooting lineage, and bears a strong resemblance to the popular pre-war Parker-Hale aperture sights. (Dr R. Maze)

no illusions that they were not facing the untrained rabble they expected, but a very efficient and well-drilled enemy who had an apparently inexhaustible number of very fine shots in their ranks. It was commonplace for Turkish snipers to snapshoot at 200yd or beyond the unwary whose faces or heads were briefly visible through small gaps in the Allied parapet. As a result, home-made trench periscopes became commonplace among the Allies during the fighting and were to later become an essential part of the trench soldier's armoury.

While there are some unconfirmed reports that German military 'advisors' brought scoped rifles to the Gallipoli front (and this is quite possible), the numbers involved would have been tiny and would have made no difference to the overall effect of sniping during the campaign. During the subsequent operations in Palestine (1917–18) it is possible that Ottoman Army troops were equipped with scoped Mannlicher M95 rifles provided by Austria–Hungary.

On the Salonika front, Allied forces faced Bulgarian troops also equipped with M95 rifles and carbines. While the author can find no images of scoped rifles in use among Central Powers forces on that front, there are some depicting riflemen firing from behind steel loophole plates and the conclusion can be drawn that like the sharpshooters of other armies with no official sniping rifles, Bulgarian marksmen made the best use they could of the standard-issue rifles.

The Germans did field some snipers in East Africa, one of whom shot and killed the celebrated British hunter and explorer Frederick C. Selous on 4 January 1917.

A newspaper image of an Italian sniper firing a Carcano rifle from a cradle mount. The reason for the use of the cradle mount is obvious when one realizes that the sniper cannot hold the rifle's butt into his shoulder because of his body armour. He also wears the impractical 6lb 5oz 'Farina' armoured helmet.

Sniping in mountain warfare

Although much of the fighting on the Italian front was along the Isonzo River, it is today remembered primarily for the extraordinarily hard mountain warfare which took place through 1916 and 1917. Aside from battle casualties through persistent shelling and sniping, many thousands of men died as a result of avalanches, bitterly cold temperatures and sudden rockfalls. Because combat ranges could vary from dozens of metres to several hundred, carbine sniping rifles were also used alongside standard rifles. Sniping rifles were in short supply for mountain troops, however, particularly in the Italian Army.

When the outside temperature was possibly –20°C or lower, frostbite was a constant companion and death from freezing a real possibility. Specially designed cold-weather clothing was supplied to Austro-Hungarian snipers, with thick felt over-boots, woollen mittens, kapok or down-lined tunics and a variety of forms of warm headgear.

The thin cold air of the Alps brought its own problems, for at high elevations the low air temperature and humidity have a considerable effect on the trajectory of a bullet and Austro-Hungarian snipers were given

Images of sniping in the Alps and Dolomites are few and far between. This one shows an Austrian sniper with a Mannlicher M95 sniping rifle in what is doubtless a posed image. The built-up timber-and-wattle parapet is typical of the fragile mountain defensive systems.

tables that allowed them to compensate for this. (Compensation for these factors required the scope elevation to be increased beyond the normal range.) Indeed, simply estimating the range from a high elevation was an

Cortina d'Ampezzo, winter 1917 (opposite)

An Austrian sniper from a Tyrolean rifle regiment moves into a recently captured position in the Alps. Many such soldiers were mountain hunters specializing in deer and goat and were extraordinarily accurate shots. He is carrying a Mannlicher M95 equipped with an Austrian-made Reichert scope. Although standard uniform was worn, in the winter cold, often below −20°C, Austrian soldiers wore a heavyweight lined *Winterbluse* wool tunic and trousers and the peaked *Kappe* was often preferred over the *Stahlhelm* as being warmer and less cumbersome.

His opposite number, an Italian sniper, lies dead after being hit by a sniper's bullet. His arm of service, the Alpini, were the oldest mountain troops in the world, with a well-deserved reputation for toughness and stamina. His rifle is a 6.5×52mm M91 Carcano, based on the tried-and-tested Mauser action, with a French-pattern 3× APX scope. He has a white cover over his M1915 French Adrian-pattern helmet, which Italy adopted in 1916. His standard uniform is concealed underneath a padded two-piece snow suit and because of the nature of his relatively immobile work, he wears heavy felt over-boots to protect against frostbite. In practice, mountain troops on both sides wore whatever they could lay their hands on to keep warm, and his long-sleeved brown leather gloves are personal equipment.

Using local materials was the most effective method of camouflage. Here, a British sniper wearing a netting face veil and ghillie suit points his rifle at the camera. His mask incorporates white cloth to match the chalk rocks lying around, and his rifle is wrapped in cloth strips. (© IWM Q 95965)

art in itself, as was adjusting for deflection due to the wind, as none of the usual methods of determining wind strength such as trees, grass or shrubs were available to use as a gauge. A flag or piece of cloth hung nearby was often the only means snipers had to determine wind strength, but this had to be used carefully as it could give away a sniper's position.

Often, the weather conditions simply made sniping an impossibility, with high winds, low cloud or blown snow blotting out the target. This explains the odd paradox of why in the mountains, shorter-range sniping at ranges less than 300yd was often commonplace. Of course, at such close ranges seldom more than one shot could be fired as retaliation, in the form of mountain artillery or machine-gun fire; but where the 'trenches' were simply no more than stone breastworks, it could be swift and deadly.

Sniping in mobile warfare

As the war continued into 1918 and fighting moved beyond the trenches, snipers on both sides began to be used more aggressively. The offensive tactics developed the Allies in 1917 were later employed to great effect during the 'Hundred Days' advance between August and November 1918, when Allied snipers were sent out in front of the advancing Allied army to pick off artillery observers and rearguards left behind by the retreating Germans.

Snipers also proved valuable in defence. On the other side of the wire the new defensive tactics adopted by the Germans paired snipers and machine-gun teams, with snipers observing for targets and dealing with any Allied infantry who crept too close. These tactics proved to be highly effective, requiring little manpower for the defenders but proving very costly to the Allied attackers; dealing with these mixed units was a priority as it required only three or four well-concealed machine-gun/sniper posts to stop an attack in its tracks. This posed a problem for the Allies, for much of the fighting was based around German defensive lines composed of lines of concrete bunkers with interlocking fields of fire. They were

impervious to artillery fire, or mass-assault, so snipers became the only means of overcoming them. The Germans were secure in the knowledge that the attackers were too far advanced to call upon their own artillery for support, so the abilities of the Allied snipers to locate and deal with the Germans assumed particular importance.

Canadian and ANZAC snipers excelled at this irregular fighting, using their fieldcraft to infiltrate enemy lines and get within sniping range. To cite but one example: at Mont Saint-Quentin on 2 September 1918, a sniper of the 25th Battalion Australian Infantry Force, Private Walter T. Chapman, saw two German machine guns being set up to enfilade his unit. He crawled forwards then opened up accurate fire on them, killing 12 men, knocking out both machine guns and forcing another 28 men to surrender. He won the Military Medal for this act, one of five won by Australian snipers that day. In dealing with the German machine-gun units and eliminating snipers countless Allied lives were saved and the momentum of the advance was maintained. The Australian snipers were later singled out for specific praise by Lieutenant-General John Monash, commander of the Australian Corps.

While many US snipers were armed with the Model 1903 rifle, the Model 1917 was also used to great effect by many American sharpshooters, despite never being issued with a telescopic sight. Possibly the most famous example was provided by a US soldier who was not a trained sniper. While on patrol on 8 October 1918, Sergeant Alvin York of the 328th Infantry Regiment engaged a German machine-gun unit with his

ABOVE LEFT
A photograph taken on active service of a British sniper wearing full marching order. On one shoulder is his scope carry-case and his binoculars are on the other. Presumably he has the bayonet affixed merely for dramatic effect! (Stephen. J. Chambers)

ABOVE RIGHT
A US Army sniper, identified as Lieutenant L. Hain of the 127th Infantry Regiment, working from a trench position with his Springfield Model 1903/Warner & Swasey M1913 combination. According to the press release, Hain had just accounted for two Germans. His rifle has the multi-purpose Pattern 1908 rifle sling, so practical that it continued to be issued in World War II. (US Army)

A very unusual photograph of a late-war German machine-gun team, with accompanying sniper. He would spot targets for the machine-gunner through his telescope and deal with any close-range threats. Note the soldier on the left wearing body armour.

Model 1917 rifle, killing 18 Germans with 18 shots (and a further nine with a pistol) and capturing 132 others, for which he was deservedly awarded the Congressional Medal of Honor.

Montfaucon, 1918 (opposite)

Neither the US Army nor the US Marine Corps possessed any trained snipers when the United States entered World War I. In part this can be ascribed to the fact that the US armed forces had virtually no tradition of sniping, having not been involved in a major conflict since the American Civil War. Yet by 1918, sniping had become an established and crucial part of warfare and the Americans belatedly did their best to adapt to circumstances. Once employed on the battlefronts the Americans proved extremely adept, many having learned fieldcraft and accurate shooting as small boys in the woods and forests of the United States.

In practical terms, there were almost no telescopic-sighted rifles available to the Americans except for the Warner & Swasey M1913 prismatic scope that the subject of this illustration is using, mounted on his Springfield Model 1903 sniping rifle. His hessian suit is locally produced and painted to match the local flora; he wears his British-pattern Brodie helmet underneath a loose sandbag cover. Unlike the British, American snipers often camouflage-painted their rifles. He wears minimal equipment – ammunition pouches, water bottle and a belt knife.

IMPACT
Lethal accuracy

An extremely rare photograph of a working German sniper wearing a *Stirnpanzer*. His protective leggings and the heavily built-up trench would suggest that he is in a very wet area, probably Flanders.

It is rarely possible to determine exactly what impact an individual form of weapon has had on warfare. Looking at one very small and specialized element of an army such as sniper units would tend to lead to the conclusion that considering World War I as a whole, they probably contributed little. Yet this is far from the case, for their impact went far beyond the actual numbers of enemy they killed, considerable though this was.

SNIPER EFFECTIVENESS

Exactly how good snipers in World War I were was of course entirely down to the ability of the individual. There are several accounts of soldiers peering over a parapet being hit by bullets fired by two different snipers. Regarding effective ranges, Hesketh-Prichard always stated that 400yd was perfect for a head shot, but he was an exceptional rifleman. In ideal weather conditions – still and dry – this should be possible for a good sniper, with a body hit attainable at 600yd. Snipers aimed at the teeth if possible, as this ensured an immediate killing shot. Moreover, if the range had been incorrectly estimated, then it would result in a head or chest hit, both equally lethal. In poor weather, however – particularly high wind – sniper instructors stated that shooting at ranges greater than 400yd was merely a waste of ammunition.

The service life of a sniper, as with that of anyone in a high-risk profession, such as combat pilots, relied on their ability to survive the first few weeks of fighting. The longer they lived and the greater the level of experience they gained, the better their chances of survival became. There was a point, however, at which a sniper's mental capacity, nerve and efficiency became seriously compromised, through fatigue, combat stress or wounds. This timescale varied from individual to individual; there are accounts of men being returned to their units as mentally unfit after only a week of sniping duty. The example of Private Thomas O. Durst is instructive. He trained as a scout sniper in 1915, and was twice hospitalized as a result of close encounters with German snipers, once, according to his medical records, with 'Bullet wounds to the head and buttock' and again with a 'Wound to the head and ankle'. Both of these wound types are synonymous with being struck while in a prone position, and he clearly felt his time as a sniper was likely to end prematurely, so in late 1917 he applied for a commission in the Machine Gun Corps. Surviving two years as a front-line sniper was no mean feat and he was fortunate to see the end of the war.

Sniping casualties

It is difficult to find any figures about how many lives were lost in World War I due to sniping, for it was generally regarded as clandestine and snipers' tallies (assuming they kept them) were seldom ever made public. As far as the author can tell, no official figures for World War I have been published, with a very few individual exceptions. The Canadian Corps did present an overview of their sniping effectiveness in a 1916 report to Canadian Corps HQ. From 1 January to 5 April, the snipers of the 1st, 2nd and 3rd divisions accounted for 406 Germans. Multiply this to the end of the war and it comes to 3,248 kills, assuming the rate of kills remained relatively static as the fighting moved into open warfare. This of course, is an official total; in practice, most snipers accounted for double the number accepted by the authorities, as only hits observed by a second person were counted as 'official' and many snipers worked alone or took shots the results of which were impossible to confirm.

A British 1917 Mk IV trench periscope with the bullet hole made by a German sniper.

To extrapolate further, consider that by 1918 the British Army had 70 divisions incorporating over 1,000 infantry battalions and each of these had its own sniping contingents. Even if only 20 men per battalion were so employed, this meant that some 20,000 snipers were available – and this does not take into account the Australian, Canadian, New Zealand or South African continents on the Western Front. Of course, the Allies were slow to start sniping, so in terms of killing effectiveness, the Germans were already streets ahead by 1915; but again, there are no figures available that the author could find giving any clue as to their effectiveness. We can surmise that as they were more numerous and better equipped the Germans' kill ratio must have been greater than that of the Allies. There is one faint clue found in accounts of the fighting on the Eastern Front, however, for which Austrian and German newspaper reports describe their snipers shooting the Russians 'like rabbits' and estimate that across the front, 500 Russians per week became casualties through sniper fire. Even if we allow for some hyperbole, half this number is still a significant casualty rate.

A close-up of the entry and exit holes. The letter accompanying the periscope sent from No. 42 Base Hospital stated: 'As you will see, I am still here, but I expect to be released soon. I was watching Jerry's lines about 200 yards away when one of his snipers hit it fair and square! It was quite a splendid shot. My eye is much better now, and I consider myself quite lucky.' The writer is identified only as 'Charles'.

A moment frozen in time on the Salonika front, as the corporal gun layer on a British artillery piece is struck by a bullet fired by a sniper. The dust from the impact can be seen to his right, against the gun shield. The rest of the crew are unaware of what has happened.

Morale effects

There was considerable truth to the Chinese proverb 'Kill one man, terrify a thousand' where snipers were concerned, for it was not simply the number of kills that made the sniper so feared; it was the psychology involved, those soldiers facing snipers knowing that a split-second's forgetfulness could lead to death. The snipers' presence created fear, resulted in excessive caution and – possibly worst of all – added an

A fine early-war photograph of three veteran German snipers. The man at the left has the scope attached to his rifle; the sniper next to him has removed his, although the mounts are visible.

DUM-DUM BULLETS

One of the great myths regarding ammunition used in World War I concerns the alleged use by snipers of factory-issued Dum-Dum rifle bullets. No country ever issued such projectiles, but there is compelling evidence that individual soldiers did tamper with standard ball ammunition. Private F. Richards noted in his autobiography (1933) that in 1914, some of the men in 2nd Battalion, The Royal Welch Fusiliers, were snipping off the tops of bullets with pliers in the belief that the enemy were already doing so, and it was merely retaliation. This was due mainly to the average soldier's lack of understanding of the power of a rifle bullet: a .303in bullet strikes with a force of 18 tons per square inch while spinning at 2,700rpm, and the resultant wounds are often horrific. In fact, no sniper would ever tamper with a bullet in this manner, as it would ruin its accuracy over any but the very shortest of ranges.

There is also good evidence, however, of Mauser bullets being reversed in their cartridge case and there was actually some technical merit in doing this. At some point the Germans had discovered that a reversed bullet could punch through a steel loophole plate, acting like a modern discarding-sabot shell. Furthermore, out to around 300yd this modification had virtually no detrimental effect on accuracy. Prior to the issue of armour-piercing ammunition, it is quite possible that some German snipers carried a small number of these reversed-bullet rounds. The author would add that during the years he lived on the Somme, he found examples of both types of round when fieldwalking.

Proof that modified ammunition was in use. On the left is a reversed German Mauser bullet, with the cartridge case cut away to show its position. It is dated 1915. Next to it is a 1914-dated Lee-Enfield round with the bullet nose snipped off. Both were found on the Somme by the author.

element of the unknown to the already precarious conditions of life in the front line, which became increasingly apparent to soldiers as World War I progressed.

Sniping even brought about changes in uniform; by the end of 1914, officers' swords had disappeared and by 1916 steel helmets became mandatory; visible rank insignia was swiftly abandoned by British and German officers, who began to wear ordinary soldiers' uniform and equipment. Officers had learned the hard way not to stand out.

FIGHTING BACK

Fire had to be met with fire, so in the British and Dominion forces, combating enemy marksmen became the job of the sniping arm, which existed as much to give reassurance to its comrades as to provide a vital fighting function. Hesketh-Prichard noted that in areas where German

COLLECTING AND SHOOTING SNIPING RIFLES

Through his working life, the author has been very fortunate to be able to handle many experimental patterns that never made it into service as well as almost every sniping rifle manufactured. Over the last 20 years, these rare rifles have become one of the most sought-after forms of longarm for collectors and an inevitable result is that prices have rocketed, outstripping those of almost any other types of collectible firearm. As an inevitable consequence, the amount of fakery has soared and there are now far more sniping rifles available on the collector's market than ever survived combat. This is particularly true of the sniping weapons of the world wars, and unless there is a cast-iron provenance, or the weapon has been authenticated by a specialist, then any example for sale at a high price must be treated with great caution. This interest has, however, spawned an entire industry of replicas, mostly surplus rifles fitted with genuine or reproduction mounts and scopes. These provide shooters with realistic and affordable alternatives to shoot that are identical to the original rifles, without risking damage to a valuable original example.

Naturally, accuracy-testing genuine sniping rifles is always subjective, as only modern ammunition is safe or reliable enough to use. The rifle bores are now over 100 years old and have suffered from time, with poor storage and minimal cleaning, so care must be taken when selecting an original for shooting. It should also be proofed to current standards, ensuring that it is safe to fire. Assuming it has a good bore, ammunition selection is an important factor as a firearm is only as accurate as its ammunition. Old stocks of military-surplus ammunition, made to wartime standards, are no longer reliable or accurate enough for comparative purposes. Using modern ammunition made to high standards, or even better, home-loaded rounds, provides one with a definite edge over the snipers of 1914–18, and can tighten a group by 50 per cent at longer ranges.

So, assuming a shooter is actually fortunate enough to be able to fire a genuine sniping rifle, what are they like to shoot? Well, there is an inevitable comparison with modern rifles, and if one is a shooter used to today's state-of-the-art technology, the initial thought is generally 'How on earth did anyone hit anything with one of these?' The optics are the main area in which improvements are most immediately and (quite literally) visible, as modern scopes provide an image that is better defined and sharper, due to increased light and coated lenses – and normally they have variable magnification. Original scopes have none of these elements.

For 30 years the author has owned a 1915-vintage Mauser Gew 98 rifle to which a 3× Hensoldt scope is fitted. The bore is very good, indicating that its provenance (it was brought to Britain as a war souvenir) is probably genuine, as few surviving sniping rifles saw heavy use. A factory-selected Gew 98 had to be able to achieve a 60mm (2.4in) group at 100m (109yd) and the author's rifle can manage a 3in five-shot grouping at 100yd, resting on a sandbag. Despite using modern ammunition, longer-range shooting with this rifle can be variable: at 300yd it can group at anything between 5in and 8in, accurate enough to hit a human target, but hardly precision shooting.

In direct comparison, a selected SMLE rifle was expected to achieve a factory 3in group at 100yd. Only about 2 per cent of production SMLE rifles were capable of this, however. The author's 1918 SMLE with 2× PPCo scope is not quite able to replicate this even with hand-loaded ammunition, but at 100yd it can manage a 3.5in group. At 300yd it would match the Gew 98's grouping of just under 8in, albeit with the occasional flyer outside. It also suffers from a common problem on this model, the shearing of the retaining screws at the front end of the mount, allowing the scope to slide forwards and off the rifle, which is disconcerting to say the least.

Shooting at a target the size of a human head – about 8×12in – with the Gew 98 and the PPCo-scoped SMLE showed them to be capable of hitting it at 200yd with four out of five shots, with each rifle fired from the prone position and the forend resting on a sandbag. On a man-sized target at 300yd, groups for both rifles were similar, between 6in and 8in. One must, however, bear in mind the ages of these rifle barrels, and note that with factory-fresh rifles, many good shots were able to pick off enemy soldiers at considerably greater ranges.

Physically shooting these vintage rifles differs little between models; recoil is little different as their weight – 8–9lb – is much the same. The weight of the trigger pull, which is always a vital element to good shooting, is generally heavier and less precise than that of modern rifles and cannot be adjusted. To provide a comparison, the adjustable trigger on the author's modern Remington 700 TMR sniping rifle is a near-featherweight 2lb. In practice, the SMLE trigger is quite good and breaks cleanly with a 4lb pull, whereas the Gew 98 has more creep and breaks at 6lb – although, curiously, the Mauser-action-clone P14/Model 1917 triggers are lighter than the Gew 98's.

The P14 is undoubtedly an inherently accurate rifle, with excellent sights, and its accuracy is better than the SMLE's, particularly at longer ranges. At 300yd, one example shot-grouped at an impressive 4.7in. Some riflemen attribute this to the left-handed rifling, which they swear is more accurate. The only real limitation for a good shot armed with a P14/Model 1917 is the shooter's ability to see the target if the rifle has no scope. The ten-round capacity of the SMLE is far more practical for a battle rifle than the five rounds of the Gew 98 or P14/Model 1917.

The Ross rifle's straight-pull bolt does take some getting used to if one is accustomed to a turning bolt, but with use it proves less awkward to manipulate when cocking, which on 'normal' rifles usually leads to the loss of the sight picture through the scope or iron sights. The triggers are usually very good, which partly explains the success of the Ross on the target range and as a sniping rifle. My own Ross has a Warner & Swasey M1913 scope fitted, which is powerful but gives the Ross a distinct list to port due to its weight, although one soon becomes accustomed to it. On a good day the Ross is capable of matching the SMLE's 2.5in-at-100yd criteria and on occasions bettering it, but test-shooting it seldom produces the same results twice in a row. The scope inexplicably loses zero, but whether this is due to recoil, the fit in the mounting rail or internal prism movement is a mystery; this was something mentioned by Canadian sniper Herbert W. McBride. The Ross is certainly more consistently accurate if the iron sights are used.

Mannlicher M95 triggers are also good and this can be partly attributed to their straight-pull mechanisms. An unscoped rifle was test-fired and proved capable of roughly the same level of accuracy as the Gew 98, but to date the author has not been able to persuade an M95 owner to allow him to shoot a prized scoped example.

The Lebel rifle is an unwieldy weapon. Its action is awkward to both cock and eject, the short straight bolt providing poor leverage and making it quite heavy to operate, and it is muzzle-heavy due to the tubular magazine. The trigger actions seem to be very variable and most suffer from excessive creep. The surprise lies in the quality of the optics, which are excellent; the 'V' reticule on the later-pattern APX scope is extremely practical to use, as it does not block out the target image. Scope-mounting systems on either the Mle 1916 or Mle 1917 are very sturdy, and it is a shame that France did not adopt a more advanced rifle that could take advantage of this set-up. Accuracy is not easy to determine, as the ammunition used during the testing was old post-1945 surplus and the author's own APX Mle 1916 could only achieve a poor 10in group at 300yd, with some bullets failing to hit. Once must hope that a new, specially selected Lebel rifle was at least as accurate as its German or British counterparts.

Springfield Model 1903 rifles are always nice rifles to shoot; their Mauser-copy actions have positive triggers breaking cleanly at around 5lb, and with a smooth cocking and ejection action. In skilled hands I think a Model 1903 could even match the SMLE for rapidity of fire (the British Army record is an impressive 25 aimed rounds per minute). The slightly more powerful .30-06 Springfield round makes itself felt with a heavier recoil than the SMLE, but provides the Model 1903 with a slightly greater range capability. The only scoped variant the author has shot was a virtually mint World War II model with a Winchester A5 scope fitted. The scope proved to be both powerful (albeit with a narrow field of vision), accurate and very easy to adjust. It looks and feels fragile, though,

and it underlines why the US Army wanted to develop a tougher optical and mounting system. While the shooting was not done to determine absolute accuracy, it produced a very good 3.3in group at 200yd using high-quality modern target ammunition, slightly bettering the SMLE and Gew 98.

The result of mounting an offset scope on an SMLE rifle. The loophole plate was designed for sights fitted above the barrel, not offset, and so the result of this War Office requirement (issued under Specification SA 390 on 4 May 1915) is clear: any sniper attempting to shoot through the loophole found himself with a perfect image of a steel plate.

A British sniper observing an enemy-occupied street in Arras, during the summer advance of 1918. His binoculars are slung over his shoulder, and he wears almost no equipment. His rifle is an SMLE with a PPCo scope.

snipers were no longer able to dominate no man's land, the men were happier and went about their duties with greater enthusiasm.

Naturally, challenging enemy sniper superiority was not an easy task, for an effective sniper was extremely difficult to locate, even for experienced observers. If the men were in trenches a favoured method among the Allied forces was to track the path of fired bullets by pushing a cleaning rod through a punctured sandbag – preferably more than one – to establish a triangulation point. If this was not feasible, then using a dummy head and carefully checking the direction of the bullet by compass was possible. Once the area from which the enemy fire was coming was narrowed down, a sniper section would take turns observing, possibly for several days, until something – the flash of a lens, a puff of dust from a muzzle, or an involuntary movement – was seen. In cases where observation simply did not bring forth a result, field artillery could be called in to shell a precise set of coordinates. One sniper section, after hours of observing, could not precisely identify where a German marksman was located, so each sniper chose a likely target in the close vicinity and opened-up rapid fire. No further fire came from the area.

It was clear that the sniper was going to remain a thorn in the side of the armies of both sides and the level of training and numbers of snipers steadily increased as the war progressed. Countering enemy sniping was far more difficult in the open warfare of 1918, where the countryside was covered with sniper-friendly sites: woods, farm buildings, abandoned houses and old trenches. It was seldom possible to use artillery, however, so snipers were assigned areas adjacent to their unit frontages and instructed to comb them as thoroughly as possible. This was costly work for the advancing snipers and casualty rates in excess of 60 per cent were not uncommon. It was far easier for the defending snipers, of course, who could fire a few shots, then melt away to new positions in the rear.

Fighting in built-up areas also posed a new problem, for no manuals had been written to cover this eventuality. On the Western Front, each side adopted their own strategy, the Germans using light machine guns from buildings to pin down advancing troops, while snipers picked them off. Gradually, Allied snipers began to devise their own methods, concentrating first on silencing the machine guns, which were generally easier to spot, by shooting at the guns themselves. With their weapons put out of action and unable to provide cover for their attached snipers, the Germans found that retreat was the only sensible policy. It was slow work for the attackers, but effective.

CONCLUSION

The widespread use of snipers on the battlefields of World War I was to prove pivotal in the chequered history of the profession, but not immediately. Although post-1919 sniping was still much derided in some military circles as 'ungentlemanly', its sheer effectiveness during the conflict could not be denied and the outmoded views of the old school of generals had been largely replaced by a new cohort of senior commanders who rose to command through ability and experience, not education and tradition. All of the victors sought to cut their military expenditure in the 1920s, however, while the armed forces of defeated Germany and Austria were forbidden to continue with many forms of warfare, sniping among them. With the trench warfare of World War I at an end, most of the combatants assumed that the danger was past and sniping gradually slipped from training schedules.

Everywhere, that is, except the Soviet Union. When Axis forces invaded the Soviet Union in June 1941, Hitler's troops were met with unexpectedly high levels of very efficient Soviet sniping, and rapidly had to devise training and produce suitable rifles to meet the Red Army not only on an equal footing, but hopefully beat the Soviet snipers at their own game. World War II would see the widespread rediscovery of sniping among all of the major powers as the lessons of World War I were consolidated and built upon, from the Ukrainian steppes to the jungles of Burma via Monte Cassino, Normandy and Berlin.

An Enfield P14 rifle fitted with an Aldis scope. Effectively a copy of the Goerz double-claw set-up, the P14 was the first overbore sniping rifle adopted by the British Army. Unfortunately, it was not accepted into service until December 1918, although the rifle without a scope proved to be an excellent sniping weapon.

A Springfield Model 1903 rifle fitted with a Winchester A5 scope as adopted by the US Marine Corps. Although too late to make an impact in World War I, many such sniping rifles were subsequently issued in the early years of World War II. (Rock Island Auctions)

GLOSSARY

BALL	Solid lead cored, copper-jacketed military bullet.
BULLET	The projectile exiting the rifle barrel.
CARTRIDGE	Properly the brass case holding the propellant, but often used to refer to the whole round of ammunition.
CLIP	A metal strip holding cartridges so that they can be loaded into a magazine.
COLLIMATE	To ensure that the telescopic sight and bore of the rifle are perfectly aligned.
CROSSHAIRS	Intersecting vertical and horizontal lines visible through the telescope. They can take many other forms, such as a thin pillar or broken lines. Also known as graticules and reticules.
DEFLECTION	The change in the path of a bullet as a result of the wind.
DRIFT	Lateral movement of a bullet in flight away from the line of the bore, caused by its own rotation or by the wind.
FIELD OF VIEW	The size of image visible through the telescopic sight. Generally, the more powerful the magnification, the smaller the field of view. Larger objective lenses provide a better field of view.
GRAIN	The measure of weight applied to both bullets and propellants.
GROUP	The area covered by a number of bullets fired at the same point. The smaller the group, the more accurate the rifle.
HIDE	A covert sniper position, usually well camouflaged.
IRON SIGHTS	The standard metal sights fitted to military rifles, usually adjustable by the shooter only for range. Also known as open or fixed sights.
LINE OF SIGHT	The imaginary line drawn from the shooter's eye along the barrel to the target.
MoA	Minute of angle: a measurement system used to determine the accuracy of a rifle. One MoA equates to 1in at 100yd, two MoA equals 2in at 200yd and so on.
MUZZLE VELOCITY	The speed at which the bullet leaves a barrel. This decreases rapidly with distance.
OBJECTIVE LENS	The lens at the front of a telescope.
OCULAR LENS	The lens at the rear of a telescope, closest to the shooter's eye.
RIFLING	The spiral grooves in the bore that cause the bullet to spin.
ROUND	The whole round of ammunition (cartridge and bullet).
SCOPE	Any telescopic sight.
SCOPE MOUNT	Rings or saddle mounts into which the scope fits, attached to the rifle by means of a mounting base.
SERVICE RIFLE	An unmodified military-issue weapon.
SET TRIGGER	A trigger mechanism having two different pull weights, one normal and one very light. Often visible as two separate triggers.
TERMINAL VELOCITY	The speed of a bullet as it strikes the target.
TRACER	A bullet containing a phosphorus compound that ignites when fired, providing a visible trace of its flight towards a target.
TRAJECTORY	The path of a bullet in flight, initially flat, then curving downwards as gravity and loss of velocity take effect.
TRIGGER PULL	The amount of force required to release the trigger sear and fire the cartridge.
WINDAGE	Originally the loss of propellant gas through loading an under-sized ball. In modern usage, the lateral drift of a bullet in flight.
ZEROING	Ensuring that at a given range, the point of aim and point of impact coincide precisely. See also COLLIMATE.

BIBLIOGRAPHY

Armstrong, Major N.A.D. (1942). *Fieldcraft, Scouting and Sniping.* London: HMSO.

Cloete, S. (1972). *A Victorian Son.* London: Collins & Son.

Crum, F.M. (1921). *With Riflemen Scouts and Snipers from 1914 to 1919.* Oxford: Privately published.

Freemantle, T.F. (1916). *Notes of Lectures and Practices in Sniping.* Leicester: Privately published.

Herbert, A.P. (1970). *The Secret Battle.* London: Chatto & Windus.

Hesketh-Prichard, Major H. (1994). *Sniping in France.* London: Leo Cooper.

Houghton, S. (2018). *The British Sniper: A Century of Evolution.* Suffolk: Swift and Bold.

Idriess, I. (1956). *The Desert Column.* Sydney: Angus & Robertson.

Knight, J. (2004). *The Civil Service Rifles in The Great War.* Barnsley: Pen & Sword.

MacDonald, L. (1988). *Voices and Images of the Great War.* London: Michael Joseph.

Maze, Dr R. (2017). 'Great War Galilean "Optical" Sniping Sights – Past and Present (1915 use and 2015 Trials)', *Bulletin of the American Society of Arms Collectors* 115: 42–50.

McBride, H.W. (1987). *A Rifleman Went to War.* Mount Ida, AR: Lancer Militaria.

Moreno, A. & Truedale, D. (2004). *Angels and Heroes.* Belfast: Royal Irish Fusiliers Museum.

Parker, E. (1924). *Hesketh Prichard DSO, MC: A Memoir.* London: Fisher Unwin.

Pegler, M. (2004). *Out of Nowhere.* Oxford: Osprey.

Penberthy, E. (1920). *British Snipers Part II.* London: The English Review.

Plaster, J.L. (2017). *Sniping in The Trenches.* Boulder, CO: Paladin Press.

Richards, F. (1933). *Old Soldiers Never Die.* London: Faber & Faber.

Sleath, F. (2020). *Sniper Jackson.* Barnsley: Greenhill Books.

Taylor, W. & Diack, P. (1917). *J.K. Forbes: Student and Sniper Sergeant. A Memoir.* London: Hodder & Stoughton.

Durst, T., correspondence with author.

Gossen, M., correspondence with author.

Randal, T., letters in author's collection.

A pre-war production Mauser sporting rifle fitted with a Hensoldt-Wetzlar 4× scope. It has a 560mm barrel fitted into a one-piece walnut stock. Many hundreds of state-of-the-art hunting rifles were commandeered by the German Army for sniping use in 1914. (Rock Island Auctions)

INDEX